PROJECT

TEAM

DATE

EMERGENT
FUTURES
LAB

Emergent Futures Lab Press
emergentfutureslab.com

INNOVATING EMERGENT FUTURES
First Edition:
Fall 2021 Prototype Edition v2
Designed by Marco de Mel Pedersen

Iain Kerr and Jason Frasca

NOTE: You have in your possession a living and evolving document. It is an ongoing experiment. We really appreciate your engagement and welcome any and all feedback. Thank you!

INNOVATING EMERGENT FUTURES

The Innovation Design Approach for Change and Worldmaking

iain kerr and jason frasca

"There is no work of invention that does not call on a people who do not yet exist"
g. deleuze

begin
anywhere,
no ideas
but in
making

"wanderer the road is

your footsteps,

nothing else;

you lay down a path

in walking"

a. machado

two final thoughts before we really begin:

First, over the years we have noticed in ourselves a habit that when we first think about innovating our minds immediately jump to thinking about all sorts of cool solutions, end products and big ideas.

We have found that this habit is *not* helpful.

Obsessing about solutions at the beginning of the innovation process *makes invention impossible* and kills the very possibility of creation.

We all have countless answers and solutions in our heads. And the creative process is often triggered by the thought of a solution.

But remember the new is really new — it does not exist until it is made — it cannot be something we already know and can describe. So our great solution — no matter how cool it is — it's not new.

As you begin the innovation process don't hold onto that imagined perfect solution or chase after making that one perfect final invention or answer to anything, *— slow down, let go of reflexive habits, embrace the strange journey of invention, let it transform you and know that the new will emerge when you least expect it.*

And the second thought: There are many forms and goals of innovation. This book does not cover all of these, it is designed with the express purpose of assisting in the process of producing innovations that open up new worlds, new ways of doing things and new ways of being alive. Thus, while other books and processes might focus on other forms of developmental creativity and invention, our primary focus is on qualitative change and worldmaking - *How to Innovate*.

get free bonus book material!

Let's be honest, innovation is hard, messy and as tangled as the headphones you stuffed in your backpack. While we've made every effort to "untangle" innovation - even our explanations require explanations. So we created bonus book material for you, our dear fellow innovator.

Wherever you see this little crow bonus book material is available on our website.

For access, grab your phone, launch your camera and snap the QR code below:

You'll be taken to an exclusive page on our website. Signup and you'll have access to all the bonus material noted throughout the book. We will be updating this regularly as we discover and invent new tools.

Addionally, you will have free access to our widely heralded email newsletter - delivered to the front door of your inbox every Friday morning. We may even throw in a few easter crow eggs for fun (we're crazy like that.)

welcome
what
comes
next

CONTENTS

other worlds are possible

"I don't know how else to talk about this other than to encourage people to experiment...

nobody knew whether things would work or not...

I think that the best way to figure out what might work is simply to do it...

One must be willing to make mistakes. In fact, I think that the mistakes help to produce new modes of organizing..."

a. y. davis talking about her activist work in the 1950s & 60s

PREFACE: INNOVATION?

WHY INNOVATION NOW?

We live in an era of large-scale radical transformations from Black Lives Matter to Climate Change to rapid technological breakthroughs — all of which exceed the grasp of our existing conceptual, social, ecological and political tools.

To truly engage with these and other novel changes we need new tools — for it is our historical tools, structures and habits that have gotten us into this reality and are unlikely to get us elsewhere.

We need innovation to help us break with what has been done — we need to imagine that the future does not need to mirror the past with only minor corrections. Today, more than ever, we need the powers of creativity and invention to open up the possibility of genuinely new futures.

That is one clear reason. For us there is another just as important and valuable a reason for becoming innovative and engaging creativity: wonder.

We live in an open and evolving universe full of creativity and ever advancing into novelty. Innovation ultimately does not "solve" anything — it coaxes transformative differences to emerge and these differences in turn change us and the world in astonishing ways.

Living actively within and of a world of change is to live in beauty and adventure. With this foremost in mind, think of creativity and invention as fundamental skills for being alive, for the flourishing of life — it is what allows all of us collectively to make new and meaningful changes in our precarious and ever changing reality.

The practices of creativity and invention are fundamentally about developing a sense of joy, curiosity, and agency within the changing nature of reality that exceeds us at every moment.

HOW?

This is no easy task: between the potential to simply improve on the past and the space of novel possibilities is an infinite qualitative gap.

Novel futures *necessarily* exceed knowing and first come into being not as something we can recognize and fully grasp *but as vague and amorphous new modes of doing, making, sensing, and feeling.*

This is the paradox of radical creativity. We can know an issue extremely well, but the new, to the degree it is truly new — *cannot be known in advance.*

This book and its approach are grounded in this paradox. Both because of this paradox, and the very real challenges we face, we need new speculative tools for qualitative transformations — we need to be able to invent problems worth having for worlds worth making.

Other worlds are possible. This is both the genesis and goal of this text.

leave
space
for the
unexpected
to sweep
you
elsewhere

USING THIS BOOK

We have named the set of tools and procedures that we outline in this book *The Innovation Design Approach* (or IDA for short). IDA is a way of approaching creativity, invention/innovation and design in general. It is an ethos, an overarching framework and a set of connected practices for producing truly novel outcomes.

It is intended to be pragmatic and applicable across a wide variety of fields from ecology to entrepreneurship, from philosophy to politics, and from basic education to advanced biology. The core focus of the Innovation Design Approach is to help you develop processes that allow for genuinely novel possibilities to emerge in the face of difficult and open-ended areas of interest.

At the heart of our ethos is our conviction that ideas only come about from doing. Reading and ideating alone do not lead to novelty. Thus, we have written a workbook and not a textbook.

For creativity to happen this book needs to be used and not simply read, and it is with this in mind that we invite you to see the purpose of this workbook as being twofold:

1. To help and teach you the key skills and tools for innovation (where our techniques act like a temporary scaffolding).
2. To support your unique innovation process no matter what phase of the process you are in.

A couple of additional thoughts:

1. As a learning tool this book is best thought of as a form of scaffolding designed to support and catalyze your learning, and because of this we do not attempt to cover every aspect or every skill needed for innovation. Our goal with this workbook is to give you a sense of the terrain and teach you a set of critical techniques and processes. Ultimately, as your skills develop the scaffolding is left behind.

2. Whatever stage of innovation you are in, we designed this workbook to help you. None of us are starting in the same place or facing the same issues. After the introduction we have a guide: How to Hack the Innovation Process, to help you figure out where to start in this workbook and how to proceed.
3. *On being practical & creative:* our goal is to assist you in experimenting collectively with the real so that the genuinely new emerges. As such our approach is entirely pragmatic. Why does this matter when redefining creativity? Being pragmatic, for us, means that all of our various claims and propositions about creativity and innovation are not intended as the ultimate definitions or final truths on the subject — but as useful tools and lures towards an experimentation that "excludes nothing" as William James puts it. Our goal is creative actions.

That said — pragmatism is never simple — in fact in regards to creativity, pragmatism needs to be skeptical of the desire for simplicity. Things are just too surprising. The philosopher who coined the term creativity, A. N. Whitehead puts it well: *seek simplicity and doubt it.*

It's not that we want to make things complicated — far from it, but *change is never simple* -- it is always deeply strange and truly confounding. The pragmatism we are espousing is one of falling in love with change such that radical surprise becomes a given — *wonderment.* Being pragmatic in regards to creativity is to embrace the beauty and a joy of aberrant leaps and qualitative shifts. For us being practical and creative means that we need to care for beauty, joy and strangeness that is fully part of the practice of change.

For us, the Innovation Design Approach is part of an experiment to develop better tools and frameworks for innovation. As such, this book is an open toolkit which we hope you will experiment and *hack* freely. This framework's utility can be judged by whether it works for you.

How will you know if it works? Try the practices, do they lead you somewhere interesting? In doing so, we hope that you will change these practices and make them your own.

So try things out: experiment and evolve things and if you like what you discover in your experiments, be in touch, share what you discover -- let's continue this experimental journey as partners.

However you proceed, please don't ignore the glossary: while we strive to use simple everyday language, there is a downside to this: we need to use common words in very specific and occasionally odd ways. The glossary is meant to help clarify our tools and concepts.

REMINDERS AS WE BEGIN:

- Get out in the world, work with many others
- Ask yourself: in what area do you wish to make a difference? Find similarly minded rebels, conspirators and collaborators. Put the book to work
- The great joy of invention is that you will change your practices, habits, outcomes and ideas many times. Welcome the change
- Develop and transform the workbook. If something is not quite right for your project — that is a good thing. This workbook is meant to be transformed. Treat it only as a starting point and scaffold
- Be playful, curious, malleable, and open to wonder
- Pause, slow down, don't immediately jump to answering the questions. Take your time, read carefully, go out into the world, engage others deeply, ask questions, and make lots of notes
- If the question does not apply or seems wrong, revise it (if possible never truly skip a question)
- Do things in order. Things build upon things
- *Do not focus on solutions* (this will only lead you away from innovation). If you already know where you want to end up — then there will be no innovation. Focus on the process. Let the solution reveal itself to you through the process
- Innovation is recursive, this means that you need to go backward and repeat steps more than once. Don't see this as a setback, it is the only way forward (really sideways — which is the new forward). If something is not working go back to the point where it was, and start again
- To get good at innovating we feel strongly that it is most helpful to apply these tools to as many aspects of your everyday life as possible. Try them at differing speeds and with differing intensities, set yourself short challenges: could you cook a meal using this process? How about design a coat?

Repetition is an amazing teacher: make hundreds of meals and thousands of variations of your daily habits

- Enjoy the process, don't prejudge outcomes, fall in love with what you don't yet understand, be moved by things. Laugh, care, and be curious about what changes you
- Be in touch

everything
begins
and
lives in
the
middle

ON INNOVATION

PART ONE: IT'S TIME TO REINVENT INVENTING

in the beginning was the detour

Before we begin engaging directly with innovation and creativity we need to pause and take a detour into the early history of these concepts in the West.

Really? Why?

(Yes, we get it, why revisit ancient history, when we are trying to get to the future! But, there really is no other way...)

we have nearly everything wrong about creativity

If we go back and uncover the logic of the early history of creativity we will see that as a culture we have nearly everything wrong about creativity.

We don't say this lightly or for the sake of being provocative. This is a conclusion that we have reluctantly come to through our work over the last two decades helping communities, academics, individuals and companies innovate across a crazy diversity of fields, contexts and situations globally.

searching for a method

Years ago, when we first started working with others to innovate, we would spend countless hours researching, testing and modifying dozens of existing ideas, approaches and systems for fostering creativity — we tried pretty much everything from Human Centered Design to Lateral Thinking and much else.

It was only through utilizing and putting these innovation approaches to the test that we came to seriously doubt all standard models of creativity, design and innovation. Quite simply they did not lead to innovation — at the most, they led to reasonably interesting variations of what we already knew. But, *real* innovation? No.

it must be something in the water

Seeing firsthand the limits of so many highly distinct models for creativity led us to realize we needed to look deeper into how we as a culture have come to define, understand and conceptualize creativity.

creativity is not part of the western tradition

Digging into the history of creativity in the Western tradition was, for us, at first profoundly frustrating, and ultimately a transformative experience that revolutionized our own approach to innovation.

What was really frustrating was *the total lack of any discussion about what we would call creativity* (the making of something genuinely novel). Going all the way back to the ancient Greeks there is simply no discussion of how humans can make something novel.

the west always understood creativity as copying

Instead what we found was a model of making via *inspiration.* Inspiration literally means: "divine guidance." Human creation was understood as following a pregiven model (God's plan) gained via inspiration (God's help), which we should then copy and make it real as best we could (God's grace). In this framework, we humans come to do novel things only by following a directive stemming from a fixed plan gained by outside intervention.

truth is antithetical to creativity

What was the content and goal of this divine guidance? From these ancient Greek beginnings, divine guidance (the muses) took the form of assisting us in uncovering a predetermined and ahistorical ideal (idea and plan).

These ideals were manifestations of *true* essences (pure ideas). And for the Greeks to be true meant it could not be *changeable* — after all two plus two cannot equal five tomorrow and still be true. Truth was something fixed and unchanging. Because it was unchanging it could not be material, tangible or part of our everyday world — for everything material in this world eventually decomposes and disappears. In the world of our everyday lives, everything changes. Thus the ideals — the essences and truths that the western tradition sought to uncover and follow were necessarily immaterial, unchanging, essential truths. And as unchanging truths they reveal a mindset in which the highest human aspiration is not in making something new or of this world but in copying perfectly something unchanging and otherworldly.

creativity: find and follow the plan

Western makers and thinkers came to see fixed essences and unchanging models everywhere. This search for hidden plans and models behind everything can be seen in Da Vinci's famous *Vitruvian Man* sketch. Da Vinci believed that humans were necessarily modeled on perfect geometric forms of the circle and the square.

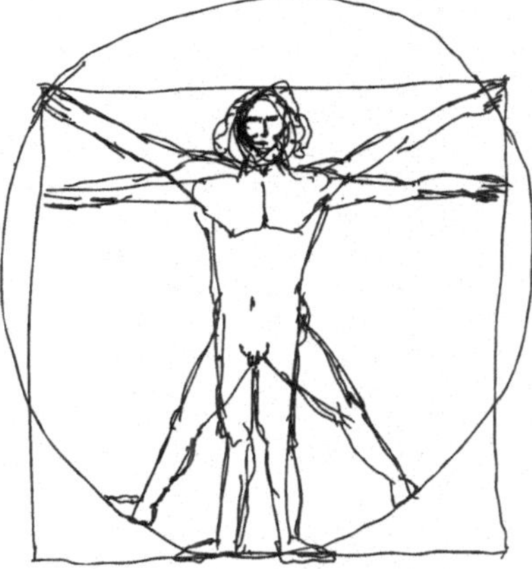

That one could define the human form with a circle, and a square showed that there was a fixed hidden plan and perfection to the universe.

While today we admire Da Vinci for what we understand anachronistically to be his innovations and inventiveness — in short his creativity — he understood himself to be doing the opposite: finding and following a timeless truth to the full degree his "genius" (the inclinations that God gave him) allowed him. For Da Vinci and the historical Western tradition, the world and all that is — is the physical realization of a pre-existing ideal or plan.

In this tradition, humans are always situated as more or less successful copiers of a pre-existing immaterial ideal or plan. Within this worldview, only God, or some form of prime mover, could be said to truly create something novel (in coming up with the ideal plan). Humans on their own do nothing genuinely creative.

ideas are everything

We are those who gain access to the "mind of God." And then once we have access these ideas flow into our mind as ideas that we can act upon.

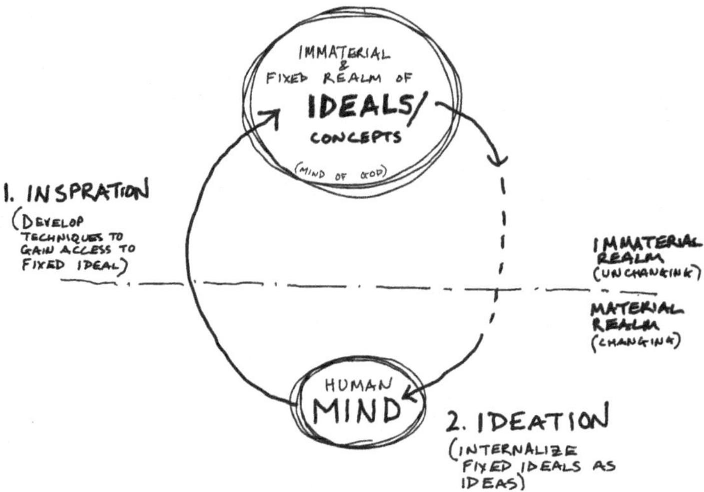

same pattern different time

It would be a mistake to think of this as simply a religious worldview, or an outdated mode of philosophizing, or a quaint, but interesting, historical anecdote. The underlying logic of this story is still very much the underlying logic of how we understand and explain the invention of things and the functioning of scientific truths:

- Everything begins as a pure idea
- It is immutable and immaterial

- This idea acts as a plan
- Carrying out these ideas as predetermined plans is how everything comes into being
- Making is reducible to the simple act of carrying out the plan
- Making is the imposition of form (the idea) on passive matter

Once you recognize this model, you will see it is everywhere:

- Physicists speak of knowing the mind of God when they discover a fundamental equation — even going so far as to imagine the existence of a singular unified theory of everything (The Plan) — that one equation that could explain everything.
- Artists and inventors talk of having a eureka moment when the plan comes to them in a single moment of vision.
- Geneticists talk about genetics as the hidden plan inside each cell that the cell follows to make the next cell based upon the genes predetermined model.

There can be no doubt that this model is very much alive and well today.

But is it the correct way to understand creativity and reality in general? Does it have any actual validity?

The simple answer is no — it is based upon outdated concepts of (1) an unchanging and closed universe, and (2) novelty springing from human minds.

Despite this knowledge our historical habits persist — we are still mistakenly looking for unchanging essences, fixed mind-based ideas and complete blueprints — and in doing so fail to see how the reality all around us is complex, highly interdependent, historically contingent, planless, and profoundly creative — with novelty emerging spontaneously where least expected.

creativity has only existed for 150 years in the west

In light of this, it makes perfect sense that the very first usage of the word "creativity" in English as a noun was only in 1875. While this might sound shocking, it is profoundly important to recognize that *we do not come from a history or tradition that has had a longstanding interest or place for genuine novelty*. And because of this, most of our contemporary ideas about creativity carry over complex hidden anti-creative habits, concepts and processes.

our models of design & making are unwittingly ancient

The inability of our current creativity models to foster real novelty makes perfect sense when you realize that they have unwittingly carried over into the present the basic logic and process of a tradition that understands novelty as ultimately unreal or as only arising from some fixed ahistorical idea.

But, understanding this fixation with fixed ideas and plans does not fully explain the power these models have held over our development of creative methods. The main force that these models have today is in the *processes* that we still use to foster creativity. These historical models of design are "God models" and their process is one in which they ask us to act like a God of creation and *to think things into being*. This process has three key steps:

1. *Ideate*

2. Plan

3. Make

But, if creativity is, as we will argue, about the emergence of *anything* novel — how can it be focused on ideation and the follow-through from this initial idea?

Do new forms of life creatively emerge via ideation?

Of course not — how could a dinosaur brainstorm its way into becoming a bird? If we look around and see the novelty of life — we know that none of this creativity followed a plan or an idea — it came about because of a complex, contingent and unthinking process of evolution (which we will investigate shortly for cues to an alternative model of creativity).

With most of our current models of creativity, we can see that they have unconsciously carried forward the classical linear model (ideate, plan, make) that never had to actually address the question of how novelty is possible because it was taken for granted that God alone created.

But with God — or any fixed immaterial ideal — removed from the picture of creativity, does this linear model still make sense?

How does this "ideate first" model account for the emergent creativity that arises in action? In materials? In environments? In evolution? In unplanned accidents?

Before fully addressing these questions that take us into the heart of real creative processes, it is important to understand how pervasive and implicit this "ideate first" model of creativity is today.

In our own research and comprehensive surveys of models of creativity — nearly every model assumes that creativity is about thinking and ideas (we will mention the rare alternatives later).

Classical creativity and design are taught as a process of developing an idea, drawing it up (as a plan to show how to make it) and then making it (or have it made).

Go to almost any design or architecture program today and you will see students presenting perfectly rendered ideas and plans for feedback.

Pick up pretty much any guide to innovation and its process will begin with Ideation.

Aren't we being far too all-encompassing? Are there not examples of design processes that do not begin with Ideation? For example, doesn't Design Thinking begin by empathizing and talking with users?

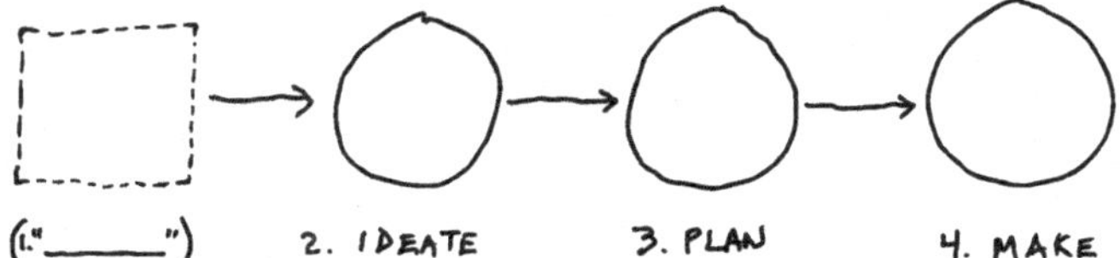

This is true, but the revisions to this process proposed by Design Thinking and other similar models keep the core model intact and simply tack on an extra step at the beginning. For example:

- Design Thinking adds Empathy
- Jeremy Gutsche adds Trend Analysis
- Equity Centered Community Design adds history and context
- Disciplined Entrepreneurship adds a customer focus
- Frame Innovation adds Frame Research
- Lateral Thinking adds techniques to loosen thinking
- The Innovators Dictionary adds analysis
- The Radical Innovation Playbook adds discovery

We encourage you to look at every innovation design method — the vast majority are basically "Ideate Plan Make"?

You will be surprised, *there really is not much else...*

While all of these tools (empathy, trend analysis, frame research, etc.) are critically important to good design — tacking these onto the fundamentally flawed skeleton of the model still leaves you with a fundamentally flawed model.

yes, but what's the flaw?

What is it that makes this three-step "ideate first" model so problematic for creativity? After all one could argue that its origin is beside the point — if it works to produce novelty.

If it works, does it really matter if it was invented as a myth?

So the question is: can the "ideation first" model produce profound novelty? There are three fundamental problems that sink this ship:

1. THINKING DOES NOT ACTUALLY HAPPEN IN THE HEAD:

on ideas and the mind of god

If we pause for a moment and just reflect on how creativity models are focused on ideation — it is in the literal dictionary definition of creativity. The Oxford English puts it this way: Creativity: "*the use of the imagination or original ideas, especially in the production of an artistic work*".

What is important here is (1) ideas are where creativity begins, and (2) ideas — thinking happens in the head.

so we are looking for a brain region?

The now almost universal assumption is that of course thinking happens in the brain and therefore we should move onto narrowing down the hunt for the source of creativity to its specific location (or locations) in the brain.

This "it's all in the head" model with its brain region focus for understanding activities like creativity has also underpinned most of the classical creativity research programs. This has led to a focus on creativity being something fundamentally neurological — a thing that can be strengthened or weakened by our habits and practices.

But, the most recent work in cognition and neurology does not support this approach:

1. The work of Michael Anderson and others on what they call "neural reuse" has definitively shown that the brain is not modular (one task - one area), but rather tasks such as seeing or speaking are widely spread across the brain and that these same areas of the brain are utilized for a huge diversity of other tasks that have nothing to do with seeing or speaking. The dream of discovering a brain region devoted exclusively to anything — much less creativity — is thus an impossible dream.
2. An even more challenging development comes from the field of Embodied Cognition: thinking cannot be properly said to occur in the brain.

What? How can that be? Where else would thinking happen?

thinking is outside the head

Of course, *our* type of thinking *requires* a brain, *but the brain alone is not sufficient for thinking.*

The brain is best understood as being functionally *inseparable* from the body-in-action interacting with the immediate environment.

Thinking does not take place in the brain — to properly understand thinking (and by extension, creativity) we need to understand that thinking happens via a coalition of brain-body-tools-environment.

the four e's (and an "a")

This approach is based upon the discoveries of the Embodied Cognition (EC) approach to mind, brain, and cognition strongly critiques the classical "ideas = representations = brain processing" model of understanding thinking.

This can be understood as the coming together of how we are *embodied, extended, embedded, enactive and affective.* This is often called the "4EA" model of cognition for short (Embodied, Embedded, Extended, Enactive & Affective Cognition).

Let's understand each of these concepts individually:

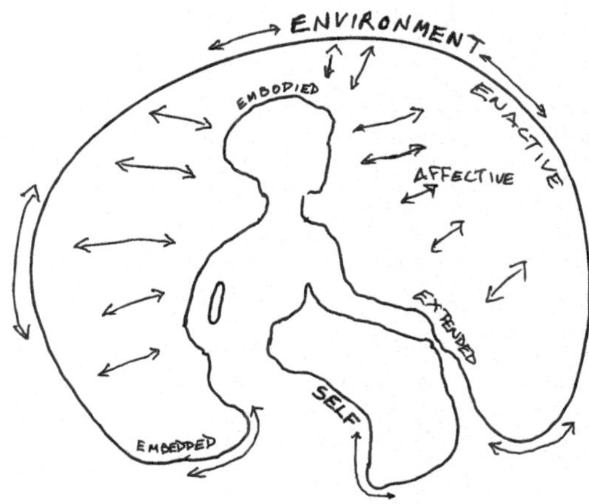

E1: embodied: Our brains are part of our unique bodies. Having the types of bodies we do — moving, grasping, sensing, and acting with specific bodies gives rise to our forms of thinking which in turn feeds back into the forming of our bodies' abilities. Practically, what does this mean for thinking? The specific types of bodies we have, and how we use them directly shapes the underlying structure of our thinking — from guiding metaphors to abstract concepts. Changing the body and changing the body's habits/actions will change how you think.

E2: extended: The kinds of thinking that we do could not happen without tools. An example: most complex math is not possible without tools: writing (symbols) plus paper and pen, or chalkboards and chalk. Today our smartphones act as extensions of our memory storing hundreds of phone numbers we otherwise would not know. In thinking the appropriate set of partners are assembled: diverse brain regions + specific embodied actions + necessary external artifacts, into a holistic coalition to carry out the task of thinking. Again, practically, this means that to think creatively we need to focus on new tools, techniques, and practices and connect them experimentally into effective novel *assemblages*. We can think of this as setting up types of labs for novelty. Tools/objects will surprise us with unintended capacities that can be discovered and followed under the right conditions.

E3: embedded: Thinking is embedded in a concrete environment and this environment shapes and patterns thinking. Chairs, rooms, houses, streets, and patterns of sidewalk and lawn might seem incidental but are fundamental not simply to thinking in general but to why our thinking gravitates towards certain patterns, logics, and outcomes.

E4: enactive: Thinking is fundamentally tied to acting — to doing where meaning arises via our actions. Meaning and thought arise during situated actions that are in a context of being co-determined along with our environment. Doing en-acts meaning into being. A cup is a cup because we use it as a cup (for containing liquids to drink), and the idea of containing arises through our specific actions of using things like cups to contain as part of a larger action such as drinking — which in turns gives rise to a model of quenching thirst which gives rise to a conceptual terrain of "thirsting" and being "quenched" — that extends far beyond actual liquids and physical needs.

A1: affective: We equate thinking with rationality, logic and high-level conceptualizing. While we do use logic — our intellectual lives and all of our thinking rests upon an emotional foundation that is continuous with, colors and saturates all experience. Experience and thoughts bubble up out of an emotional atmosphere — tone — that is our most basic sense of being alive. Most of the time we are not even aware of this emotional (affect) shaping our thoughts — emotion is working at a subconscious and minimally conscious level. And then when we are called upon to explain our actions or thoughts we skip right over the role of emotion and jump right to "reasons and logic" most of which have little to do with the actuality of our experience, decision making or thinking. Understanding this is critical to creativity and we will go into this in detail in the next section.

How does all of this help us be creative? Anderson says it best, "we are [embodied] social environment-altering tool users. Tools give us new abilities, leading us to perceive new affordances, which can generate new environmental (and social) structures, which can, in turn, lead to the development of new skills and new tools, that through a process... of scaffolding greatly increases the reach and variety of our cognitive and behavioral capacities" (Anderson, p. 182).

And this is far removed from a world of brainstorming and other techniques of pure thinking and ideation — which is very good, because:

2. THE NEW IS UNTHINKABLE: THE CREATIVITY PARADOX

Here is where the central problem lies with ideation first models of creativity: the modes of thinking that ideation relies on are high concept and representation dependent. They are most often inductive or deductive forms of conceptual reasoning. And these concepts pre-exist the activity of ideation and fundamentally shape it. Ideation is thus inherently tied to the past and what already exists. And if it already exists it cannot be considered to be novel, which means: *ideation cannot directly lead to novelty.*

Ideation, and thinking in general, is by its very nature a fundamentally conservative activity.

Put bluntly: if something is genuinely novel it cannot at first be conceptualized. Radical novelty at its birth is a-conceptual and non-representational. Humans cannot independently think their way to the new, therefore the whole Western edifice of three-step "ideate first" model of developing novel outcomes falls apart: starting with, and focusing on, ideation will never lead to genuine novelty. And moving through a linear sequence of Ideate, Plan, and Make is logically antithetical to creativity.

Does this mean thinking and idea generation have no role in creativity? Of course not. Ideas matter. But it is a question of when, in what form, and in relation to what other ongoing activity. We like to say:

No Ideas But in Making.

But that's just the beginning of it. Now let's turn to the third fundamental reason our classical model of Ideate, Plan and Make cannot work:

3. REALITY HAS A LIFE OF ITS OWN

It is not only ideation that is the problem. The process of three steps of Ideate, Plan and Make — and their sequence is deeply flawed.

First, these methods put all the emphasis on creativity as occurring solely at the initial stage of Ideation (after which you are just making the creative idea real via a plan and method of production). We now know that ideation cannot lead directly to novelty, thus having a model in which after novelty is ideated all that is left to do is "carry it out" will certainly never get to a genuinely creative outcome.

but, i ideate, plan and make all the time!

Now, of course, you can have an idea, develop a plan, and make it real. That is not in doubt. We all do this every day:

I have an idea for a cup of coffee every morning, I make a quick plan to boil water in a kettle and grind some coffee, get a filter and make my coffee. No big deal: Ideate, Plan, Make.

But the question is: will this process get you anything creative and novel?

My idea to have coffee, and the carrying out of this plan travels a highly developed and far from the novel path. We cannot confuse a process that works in everyday life to simply get known things done with the process to get anything realized.

From the perspective of creativity, this process which puts all creativity into the first step of ideation and then relegates to the rest of the process the mere realization of the plan makes the fatal error of *assuming that the world is passive and has no creative impact on our designs*.

all creativity collaborates with the agency of things and environments

The classical way we tell the stories of great inventions and the emergence of new creative practices is to talk exclusively about the people involved, their ideas and their struggles. But almost nothing is said about the objects, materials, tools and environments involved.

Equipment of all kinds has surprising powers to shape outcomes and plays a fundamental role in innovation. What do we mean by "powers"? Put simply we mean that *things shape us.*

Contemporary studies of cognition have shown that the objects (and environments) we use, fundamentally shape and transform our thinking. Tools and their use rewire our brains, change our muscles and skeletons, remake our organs, make new patterns of thought, change our sense of self, and as Marshall McLuhan argued "leave no part of us, or our culture, untouched or unchanged."

Objects don't merely support or extend existing human capacities but *fundamentally transform us*: we are what we use. Obvious examples: how smartphones have transformed us, less obvious but perhaps more profound are the tools that we almost never notice such as our alphabet.

This is not an argument critiquing technology, far from it — *to be human is to use things — lots of things* and these things that we make and then use change us and this has always been the case. What matters is that we recognize that the things we make in turn make us, this is especially critical as innovators — we are not merely making things that solve problems but we are always making new things that change us and our surrounding environment to such a degree that new worlds emerge.

If creativity is not all about ideas or reducible to the human then we have to turn to *things as our partners in experimentation and invention*: *Making is thinking* when we allow things and environments to shape us as we shape them. In experimenting (as well as puttering, playing, tinkering, improvising, etc.) the agency of things comes into play:

When a carving knife meets a piece of wood, the wood — its uniquely organized form of matter — tells us things: I will split along the grain, I can bend, if you do this I will snap...

It is in this meeting space of action that vague hunches form: "what happens if...?" Here a kernel of a very local idea forms out from the midst of acting and it leads on to follow the material and the practices further. Vague thoughts form in making: *no ideas but in making* — and these nebulous thoughts do not act to impose plans from on high but ask us to experimentally stay in the messy mix of things and follow an emerging practice in which other ideas might emerge. Who is having these thoughts? Am "I" the author? *They are authored by the event.*

The "idea first" model of creativity and innovation imagines that matter is something passive, and that ideas in a God-like manner forcefully shapes this semi-arbitrary matter into whatever we imagine and deem it should become. But matter, stuff, things - have never been passive. Matter has propensities that come to the fore depending on how we engage with them and in this way form (what we want something to become) cannot be separated from the forming power of things as processes (splitting, bending, cracking, hardening, swelling, etc.).

The history of human invention shows us that most often the so-called great inventors were not great intellectuals purely ideating their way to novelty at a desk — they were most often the opposite: skeptical self-taught tinkerers who were most comfortable collaborating with materials and letting vague aesthetic feelings lead towards the emergence of speculative imaginings via experimental forms of deeply engaged probing, testing and making over an extended period of time.

They experimented and noticed that wood if steamed bends along its grain. Metal heated and then rapidly cooled will be far harder than a metal left to cool naturally (anealing). Add the mineral Kaolin to clay and it will become almost as hard as rock when fired (porcelain).

When we do things with things they come alive and speak by revealing emergent properties.

Experimental engagement and not abstract ideation.

Rather than complaining about uncooperative assistants and the right material not existing and retreating to pure visionary ideation — novelty emerges from the middle of puttering, playing, testing, experimenting, probing, noticing, and following.

This is not simply at the level of craft and object making — social change deals with systems far too complex and dynamic for any form of linear action to work. In complex systems, outcomes are by definition unknowable. Collaboration, probing, following, coevolving and emerging are the only possibilities.

It can be argued (as we will later in this text) that all creativity comes from reality resisting our ideas. All human creativity surfs and takes advantage of some unintended (non-ideated) possibility of action (a plan)

So why are we not designing for and with the unintended?

After all, evolution does...

Why are we not working with things, environments and communities directly?

so, in a nutshell:

What is so wrong with our classical models? For us, there are six fundamental errors to the western model of creativity.

The six errors:

1. Creativity is practiced as being fundamentally about ideas and ideation
2. Creativity is developed as a linear process (even if it loops occasionally)
3. Creativity is envisioned as something that has an essence and that can be reduced to a moment (Reductionism/essentialism)
4. Creativity is instantiated as the imposition of a predetermined form on a passive matter
5. Creativity is defined as primarily a human capacity
6. Creativity is understood and researched as an internal brain state

There is much to say about these errors and we will get into them as we articulate an alternative vision of creativity.

But this is getting ahead of the story, once we came to recognize these debilitating errors we saw them everywhere — and we came to realize that almost every contemporary method for creativity exhibits more than a few of these errors. This should come as no surprise as these concepts hang together as a package. They form our implicit unquestioned paradigm of creativity: this is the human-centered, brain-based, ideation-driven, anti-process, and anti-materialist paradigm of creativity that we in the West have inherited from an almost three thousand-year tradition.

Yes, it is not a simple or recent error — even a superficial glimpse at the literature on creativity will lead one to see that these are deep long-held widespread views encompassing the Western traditions going back to the classical Greek and early Christian thinkers. We have some deep — really deep habits that we have to work our way out of, as we build new habits of creativity.

WE REQUIRE A WHOLLY NEW APPROACH TO CREATIVITY

To us, in light of these realizations, it is quite clear that today much of how we as a culture understand creativity and innovation seems profoundly misguided.

The point of this critique is not about getting history right or critiquing others — the goal is to pragmatically and effectively understand and foster creativity and ultimately powerful and necessary innovations. To do this we need to understand that part of why creativity is so hard to enact and to teach is *because we are still implicitly using anti-creative models, frameworks, concepts and assumptions*.

In our own work, we have come to learn the hard way that our historical Western paradigm of creativity *is anti-creative* and based on a series of false assumptions about reality, ideas, humans, brains, the world around us and creativity itself. For us, the consequences of these fundamental errors mean that we require a wholly new approach to creativity.

challenging the western paradigm

Now, lest we give a false impression: it is not that these models have not gone unchallenged, in fact, there are alternative concepts -- the issue is that these alternatives are not part of the mainstream discourses of design, innovation or creativity. To develop new approaches to creativity and innovation one has to wander far from the usual haunts of design and creativity.

Our own deep frustration with the historical western model of creativity led us to work with researchers in a wide variety of fields. We worked with evolutionary theorists, systems thinkers, embodied cognition researchers, ecologists, urban planners, complexity scientists, non-Western philosophers and practitioners, material science researchers, social activists, political scientists, anthropologists, and historians. We know from:

- *Embodied Cognition* that our brains are neither disembodied nor idea centric
- *Evolutionary Theory* how creative novelty emerges across all life via the co-option of unintended potentialities
- *The Material Sciences* that there is a profound level of agency in all things
- *Process Philosophy* puts creativity at the heart of all existence
- *Complexity Science* that novelty can emerge in irreducible manners from systems themselves
- *Non-Western Traditions* that there are many important alternatives

While our doubts and frustrations led us to connect with researchers in a wide variety of fields to try and understand why these models did not work — we still had to develop alternative concepts and practices. After many years, we have slowly, via trial and error, come up with a handful of powerful alternative approaches. With every passing year and every new project, we have tried collectively to evolve these techniques and propositions further. This work on an alternative model of creativity has led to this set of alternative propositions for creativity.

what is creativity?

To begin we need a working definition of creativity. Let's start really simple:

Creativity involves the emergence of novelty.

Now novelty might sound like a trivial word, but novelty means that something new has emerged, and this is profound. The new is different.

Newness is achieved when something genuinely different than what previously existed appears.

creativity has two forms: qualitative and quantitative

Innovation and creativity are about doing something new. The new involves making a change from the past — a difference. But not all forms of change, difference or newness are the same. Most often when we encounter change it is a small change to something that already exists. Perhaps it is an improvement, a minor adjustment, or extension of its functionality. Making a car go faster or more fuel-efficient are examples of this. This type of "problem-solving," that makes something better, is a form of developmental change.

But, is all change of this kind?

No, things that are radically different are not simply improvements, they are entirely different and totally novel approaches to reality.

Thus we can say that there are two distinct forms of change:

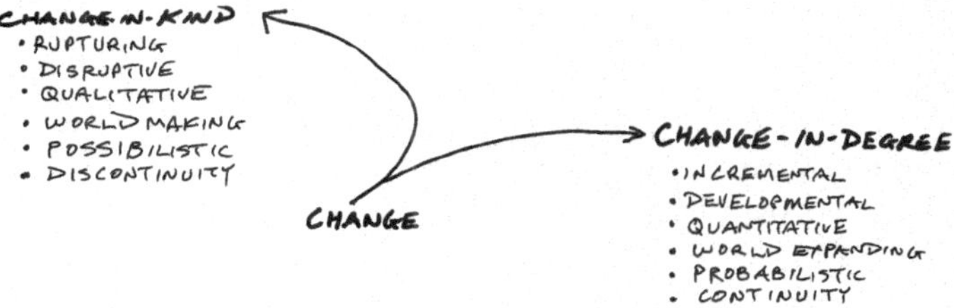

1. developmental
2. disruptive

In philosophy, these two forms of change are referred to as:

- Change-in-degree
- Change-in-kind
- Change-in-degree is: incremental, developmental, quantitative, world expanding, and probabilistic.
- Change-in-kind is: rupturing, disruptive, qualitative, worldmaking, and possibilistic.

For innovation and creativity, what is important is that:

1. Each form of change is a totally different creature
2. Each needs a different approach.

creativity involves a looping between kind & degree

While each form is quite distinct (qualitative vs quantitative), and each requires different techniques and approaches to be properly engaged — they are neither in opposition nor totally separate. All forms of change are connected in a type of double loop: push a quantitative/developmental change far enough and it crosses a threshold and becomes a qualitative/ disruptive change, and vice-versa: every qualitative/ disruptive change needs to develop incrementally to be fully realized.

For example, if you slowly and incrementally enlarge a coffee table, it will become a dining room table, and if you kept on incrementally enlarging this it eventually would turn into a simple open shelter. The incremental shift from coffee table to dining room table is a change in degree: we are still dealing with tables. But, when we continue enlarging a table and it becomes a shelter — now they are categorically and functionally totally different, one we sit at, while the other shelters us from the environment.

Thus we have *incrementally* crossed a category threshold and gone from a change-in-degree (the two tables) to a change-in-kind (tables to shelters). We diagram this by transforming our original drawing of two opposing arrows into a closed double loop. This looping two-directional diagram and logic underlies the Innovation Approach.

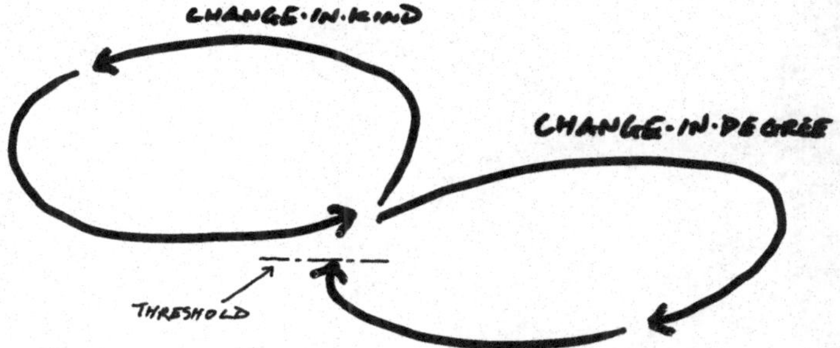

While that is a good start to understanding creativity as two forms of change or difference, we need to go further with this definition:

Creativity is the *process* of the new coming into being.

It is not enough to talk about outcomes — of changes in degree or kind — we want to know *how* to get there!

How we get there is via a process.

Creativity is about processes of change, the development of differences and the emergence of the new — that is creativity: the process of the new happening...

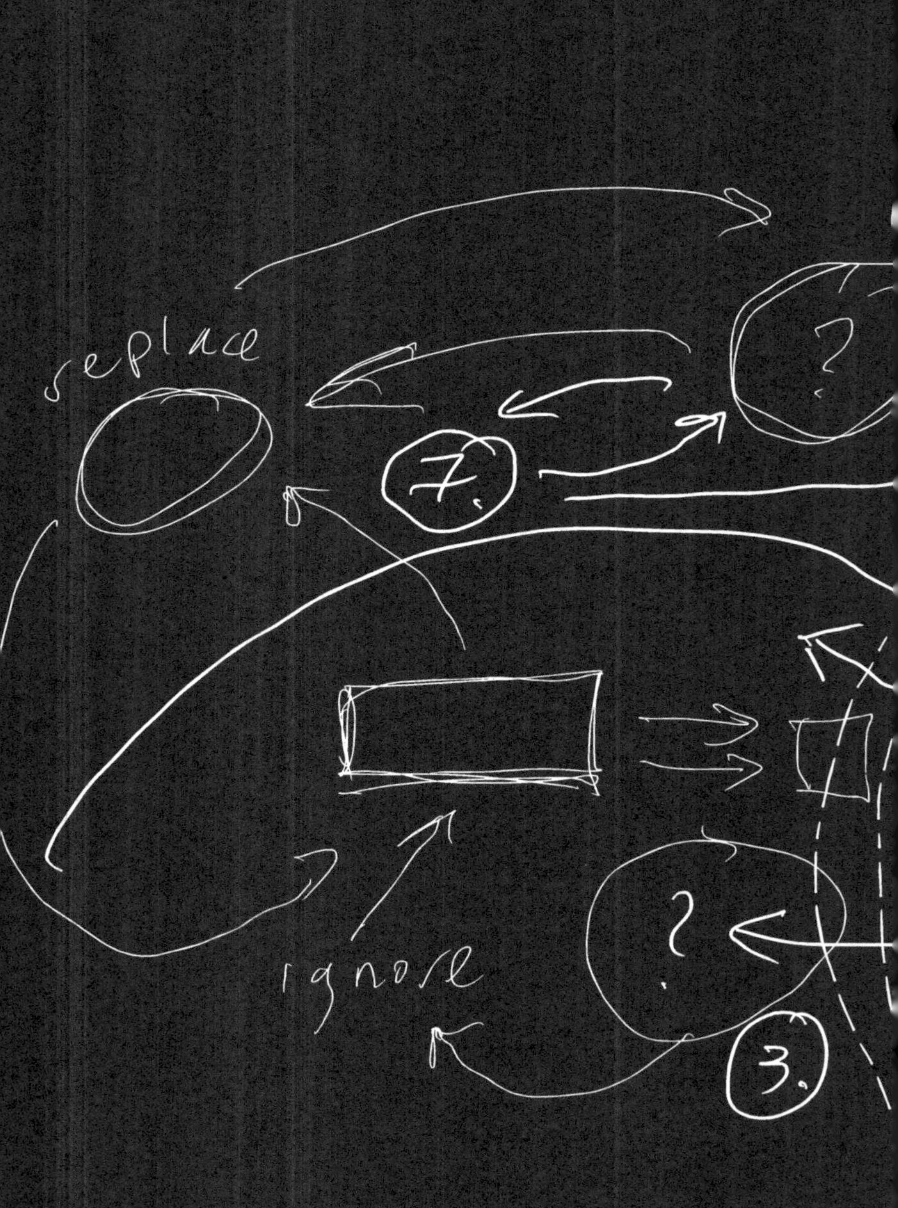

replace
?
7.
ignore
?
3.

engaged
curious
speculative
collaborative
actions

move

PART TWO: REORIENTATION

With our newfound awareness of the pitfalls of our historical model of creativity, and a sense that a new way is possible — we can now begin to develop an alternative approach. This reorientation requires reframing creativity, developing a new conceptual understanding, and developing new practices.
Let's begin:

creativity is a worldly event

When we talk in general about inventions and creativity most of us would assume we are talking about some*one* who came up with a great idea who invented something. *Why?*

There are two important issues that radically curtail and derail our understanding of creativity:

1. we assume that creativity is a human activity, and

2. that creativity is an individual activity.

Let's begin with this latter point. *Why do we assume that creativity is individual?* Why do we so quickly get to the point where we are asking *who invented this?*

In so many of our stories of creation and innovation we keep trying to discover the discreet origin, the singular source, and the ultimate *human* inventor, author, or maker — and it is only once we claim to have found this *singular source* do we begin our explanation of creativity and invention.

it's not about individuals

Pick up any book on creativity and innovation and notice how we as a culture are forever talking about "creatives" — those heroic individuals, with their special brains, and their unique essences. From Archimedes to Steve Jobs there is always someone (and ultimately someone's brain) behind everything new.

There is a fatal problem with this approach of connecting complex creative events to singular (human) sources: *nothing is ever so simple*; we now know that

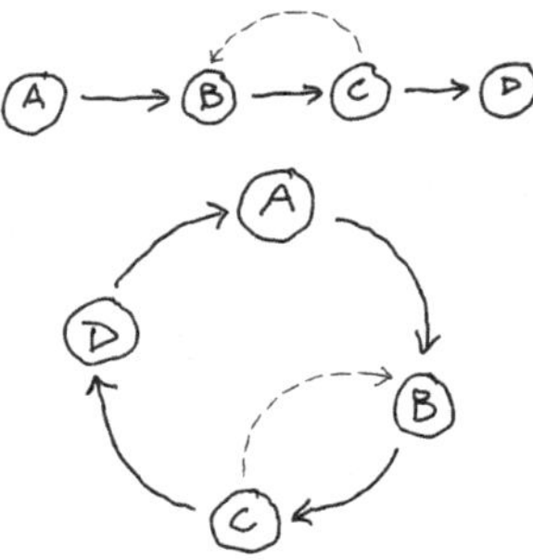

TWO LINEAR FRAMEWORKS

causality is not linear. In every moment and in every event countless factors and forces are involved in very unpredictable manners — and countless other possible outcomes could have happened. All of these factors are non-linear, indirect, contingent, emergent, multi-scalar, collaborative and irreducible. *Even the simplest moment of reality is a shit-show of complexity, and it is never possible to reduce this to a singular origin.*

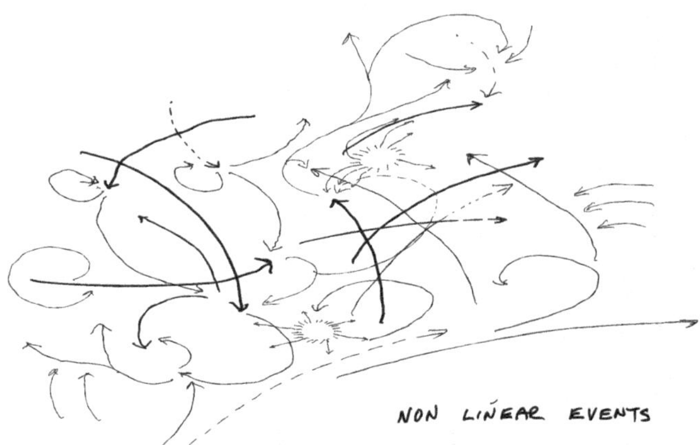

NON LINEAR EVENTS

A counterargument is often made: yes everything is complex but only *that specific* individual at that specific moment had that idea — while many others were in similar circumstances but they did not come up with anything novel and therefore it must be something unique about that person. But, this is to both misunderstand and dismiss complexity and emergence: you cannot separate a person from all the other forces that collectively make up a unique event. It is the *holistic* uniqueness of the *event* and not the individual that gives rise to the outcome.

Once we realize this, we can take a pause on our ego-driven stories of creativity and invention. We can let go of the simplistic idea of linear frameworks and heroic individualism — they have led us totally astray for far too long. The closer we study inventions and creativity the more we will see that *things have no singular author, are not invented in one singular moment, nor stem from a founding idea*. Creativity is always the synergistic emergent outcome of a complex set of factors. This insight is a complex one based on many other insights: understanding emergence, how complex systems work, and the agency of things for example — all of which we get into in this essay.

why does this matter?

Why does it matter that we put aside our heroic individualism and quest for singular sources?

To understand and more importantly *to be creative we need to be humble enough to see that no one "invents" anything or is "creative" separate from a complex messy world of forces that are just as much — if not more — the "author" than us*. And if we wish to be *involved* in creativity we need to figure out how to work in harmony *with and become part of* this complex emergent association of forces.

creativity is a more-than-human process

We can take this idea of a messy world of forces having untold emergent effects further: perhaps the most important and wondrous aspect of creativity and innovation is that *reality in all of its aspects is creative*.

Novel plants are evolving, whale songs are changing, solar systems are forming, octopus intelligence is mutating, the Black Lives Matter movement is transforming how we develop city budgets, smartphones are rewiring brains, and slime molds are inventing totally new solutions to mazes. Everywhere we look creativity is happening.

Creativity and invention are not exclusively -- or even mainly, human practices (and certainly not simply psychological). The contemporary understanding of creativity needs to fully embrace this insight: Human-driven innovations emerge from within a reality where at every moment "something" is doing something wondrous and new *without an author or a plan*. We create in and with a world in which complex systems are spontaneously self-organizing, evolving and doing new and unique things at all scales. Bird wings and dragonfly wings are astonishing acts of invention and creativity, as are cell walls, and bacteria signaling...

The new bubbles up out of a chaos that haunts, overturns, and enlivens all forms of stable order.

an interlude on processes

Before moving on, let us dwell briefly on this all-important word: *process*. Far too much of how we talk about invention and creativity involves a heavy focus on things (outcomes) — nouns — and far too little attention to the dynamics of the situation: the coming into being and changing — processes and the unpacking of verbs.

Even the most seemingly stable of things — a hammer for example is a *process*: when we look at it we see wood and metal — two very solid and stable things. But, they too are dynamic processes: trees growing and minerals being pressed into forms deep within the earth for eons are processes. And from this tree the process of crafting and form giving to the handle is a process — equally the smelting and working of minerals into metals and hammering those into the head are processes. The hammer then goes to work — it is part of the processes of making — making with nails, planks, trained arms and eyes, homeowners with dreams, cultures with patterns. If we zoom in further we see subatomic particles moving in relational processes, if we zoom out we see processes of building, and if we look to the side we see yet more processes of trees turning into planks, builders going to school, and much else besides.

In every direction, we see ongoing processes. To be attuned to creativity is to be tuned to change and *to be tuned to change is to feel and live processes*. Change happens and creativity happens because we change processes.

creativity involves attunement to realities ongoing inventiveness...

Once we understand these intertwined concepts (creativity is a worldly more-than-human process) it makes no sense to talk of creativity as having a singular author, or being an internal human property.

Now, for many, this might feel interesting but beside the point — *"sure the world is also creative, but how are humans creative?"*

Which is a fair point, if creativity is an environmental and *worldly* phenomenon then our practices of creativity cannot be thought of as being in a separate realm. Human creativity is the skillful *participation in and collaboration* with dynamic systems and emergent phenomena.

Thus human creative practices are first and foremost processes of *active attunement and experimental engagement* with these complex worldly events of ongoing creativity. We are less the originators than the skillful joiners and participants in journeys that will shock all of us. To love and become actively creative is to shift our senses from a focus on the self, ego, or any one thing, to an emancipatory vision of ourselves swimming in, carried forward by and changing in response to a vast creative engaged open-world bubbling with inexplicable novelty.

Actual novelty, as we can see, challenges some of our most basic assumptions — challenging both who we think we are, what the things around us are capable of, how change happens, and where creativity is located in all of this.

If novelty and creativity are to be found everywhere in everything — then it is important to understand what we mean by "everything". To ask about everything is to ask fundamental questions about what is real, what is experience(d), and what counts. Reality is everything that has an effect.

TRAFFIC LIGHT

what can it do? on affordances

In our innovation workshops, one of the first things we do is show participants two pictures: one of a normal everyday nutcracker and the other is of a busy intersection with traffic lights and cars.

Then we ask them: *are these two things the same?*

At first, participants are hesitant to answer — the scenario has the set-up of a trick question, and who wants to fall for a stupid trick...?

But then the answers come:

"Obviously they are superficially the same — both are made of atoms", "Clearly they are designed for quite different purposes."

Both Yes and No could be correct answers.

But, we don't stop there:

Why would we ask such an obvious question at the beginning of an innovation workshop? What are we trying to get at by asking you this question?

From this prompt inevitably a participant will suggest some use or effect that the two things have: *they both crack things. One cracks other cars and the other nuts.*

And that's when things get interesting! One intentionally cracks things and the other unintentionally. If we ignore intentionality both have a similar effect.

Then we return to our original question: *are these two things the same?*

Which prompts a wormhole of semantics to open up. In the midst of this craziness, we show a new image: A crow sitting on a powerline.

It turns out that some crows use intersections to crack nuts. They use powerlines as perches, wait for the light to turn red and the cars to stop. They then swoop down and place nuts in front of the car tires, and then return to their perch. The light turns green, the cars crack the nuts, and then the light turns red and everything stops allowing the crows to descend and eat.

From the perspective of innovation, *it does not matter what something's identity or designated purpose is*, all that matters is: *what can it do? What does it afford?*

be like a crow

It is more productive to not assign purpose, essence or identity to things but to look at what they can "afford" in relation to the situation.

Affordances are the emergent possibilities of a total situation. When cars, traffic lights, roads, trees, and crows come together in a specific manner the situation affords the crow the novel creative possibility of nut-cracking.

"Be like a crow": don't fixate on purpose, intentions or identity — rather start using things in novel ways to discover what all else they might afford. But don't stop at one possibility — keep experimenting to discover more and more non-intentional possibilities.

For us, becoming a crow is to realize that:

1. nothing is reducible to its seeming purpose or intention
2. the discovery of new possibilities can only happen through our experimental *use*.

Developing a way to "be like a crow" — a "crow becoming" so to speak is a critical first step of innovation.

from "what is it?" — to "what can it do?"

We, as innovators, are ultimately simply interested in affordances and effects and working with these to have a novel effect on something. We wish to judge things not by "what they are" in perfect isolation — but by what they afford and what effects they can produce in specific circumstances.

Not "what it is" — but "what can it do"...

But this never stops: "And what else can it do?" — This question keeps repeating as novelty emerges in experimentation...

And what all else is possible?...

creativity works with any and all effects:

From this crow perspective into creativity, *reality is everything that has an effect.*

But *what is a "thing" in this case when we say*

"every-thing"?

Is a rumor such a "thing"?

How about a delusion?

Are these the same as a hammer?

Or a political movement?

Of course, a delusion is different than a hammer — that is not in doubt, but is a delusion any less *real* for being judged untrue? While these are very different types of things (false ideas vs physical tools), *they all have equally real effects.*

If all of these effects lead directly to change — *why would we consider any of them less real or less important?*

why does this matter?

If we begin thinking about creativity only after parsing out and ignoring most of reality because it could be characterized as merely subjective, or false we both miss how reality is and how we can have an impact on it.

The question needs to be "what can it do?" not "what is it and is it really real?"

The former question is an experimental one — it is about doing, testing, noticing, following, and ultimately creating the new.

The latter is about adjudicating reality from a distance — and this offers creativity nothing. Rather it continuously reinforces only what already exists and is well and properly defined.

Experience — that sense of what something is for someone in some context (the world of affordances) cannot be separated from reality.

Following William James, and his definition of radical empiricism, we propose an alternative starting point for defining the real from the perspective of creativity: "To be radical, empiricism must not admit in its constructions any element that is not directly experienced, *nor exclude from them any element from them any element that is directly experienced"*.

Put simply, *reality is everything that has an impact.*

Experience both feeds back and feeds forward into reality.

For us as change-makers interested in creativity, this is where we begin:

We are not concerned with determining once and for all what is really really real — but only in determining what has an impact — what produces an effect — what some-thing affords — for everything that has an impact is precisely what is going to impact creativity and invention.

All "things" (objects, concepts, systems, habits, collaborations) have their own emergent transformative powers and *perspectives*.

back to the crows!

creativity surfs unintended possibilities

What Crows understand about how to engage with reality is also one of the secrets to all novelty: *The unintended is at the disruptive heart of all novelty.* It is no exaggeration to say:

All radical forms of creativity utilize the unintended possibilities of a system or a thing. A quick perusal of the history of human inventions bears this out:

- The computer: a knitting machine
- The Internet: Originally a closed communication system for the military
- GPS: developed to track satellites
- Antibiotics: uncleaned lab equipment
- The lightbulb: the early filaments were threads, paper and bamboo
- Plastics: a shellac replacement for wood
- Viagra: a heart medicine

This list is infinite — every disruptive innovation involves the unintended. But it is not just human inventions that involve the unintended — all creativity from the big bang to the flight of birds is a story of unintended possibilities being activated. Given that things have agency to shape us, it follows that they also have unintentional agency to shape us otherwise than expected.

this is how we step away from the creativity paradox

If the first part of the answer to the innovation paradox is that creativity does not begin with ideas but highly engaged actions and vague feelings, the second aspect is that creativity does not require a pre-existing conceptual plan to be realized because *it begins with a radical act of repurposing a previously existing something for an unintended, and most often unrecognized, end.* This repurposing can be a simple functional shift or utilization of an unintended aspect of the design.

We see this repurposing most clearly in the biological evolution of features such as eyes, wings or feet. Neither feet, wings nor eyes initially evolved for their current use -- this use was an unintentional development arising out of a previous quite different use.

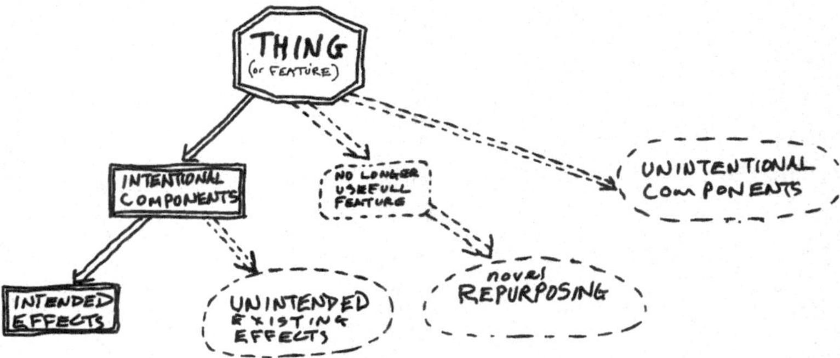

A classic evolutionary example of unintended shifts in function involves the story of how fish migrated from the sea to land. For this to happen fins had to evolve into feet. This has been a vexing question of Evolutionary Historians for quite some time. Originally it was thought that environmental changes propelled this process: water bodies were drying up and shrinking so for fish to survive the ones lucky enough to randomly have stronger fins would drag themselves between ponds. Slowly the environmental necessity to crawl on land propelled a change and bit by bit fins turned into feet while crawling on land.

This neat explanation turns out to be another false just-so story: feet do not finally emerge late in the story on land — feet evolved early in the story *in the ocean*. Who needs "feet" in the ocean? Clearly, they helped with swimming and many other non-walking activities. Feet-like fins are simply one of a vast array of aquatic propulsion strategies that emerged in the ocean.

Feet for swimming had the unintended capacity to do many things: they could help fish linger invisibly on the bottom and spring up to ambush prey, they could help fish navigate underwater grasses without giving away their location, and much else besides. Long feet and arm-shaped protrusions proliferated on diverse fish species along with other evolutions such as their eyes moving toward the tops of their heads (to see airborne flies).

But why go on land? There is no one answer, but we know with certainty it was not because of environmental change. One interesting possibility is the juvenile footed fish "escaped" briefly onto land to avoid predation and discovered they had unintended capacities to survive briefly out of water.

The french "detournement" — rerouting or hijacking is an ideal term for this *process*.

detournement — it's a process, not a concept:

While the general concept is critical, it is the detailed process that once understood abstractly can be applied to the development of a new innovation approach.

If we were to zoom in on this process we would see that it is composed of a series of pivots in purpose.

"purpose is a porpoise" (bpNichol)

Everything has a purpose in relation to someone doing something (an agent, an activity, and purposeful things). The traffic light is like this: if drivers are the agents and driving is the activity, then the traffic light serves the purpose of organizing the flow of traffic to avoid accents and keep things moving. But "hovering" around or "haunting" this purpose are infinite immanent and emergent unintended possibilities awaiting a literal realization and production in use. The crow does this and a new purpose emerges: nut cracking. But this is a one-time event.

Tracking our evolving fish, the story reveals a more complex process. A key aspect of the fish to land transition is the fin to foot transformation, and the heart of this is the story of the evolution of cartilage and bone.

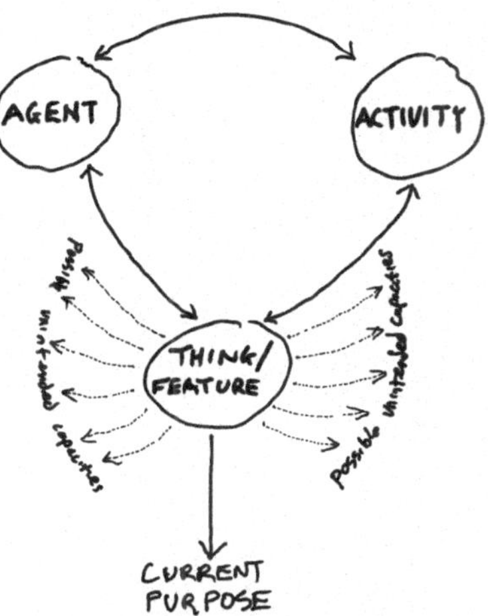

AGENT
ACTIVITY
THING/
FEATURE
possible unintended capacities
possible unintended capacities
CURRENT
PURPOSE

Following the Unintended (part 1): The relation between agents, activities and features (above)

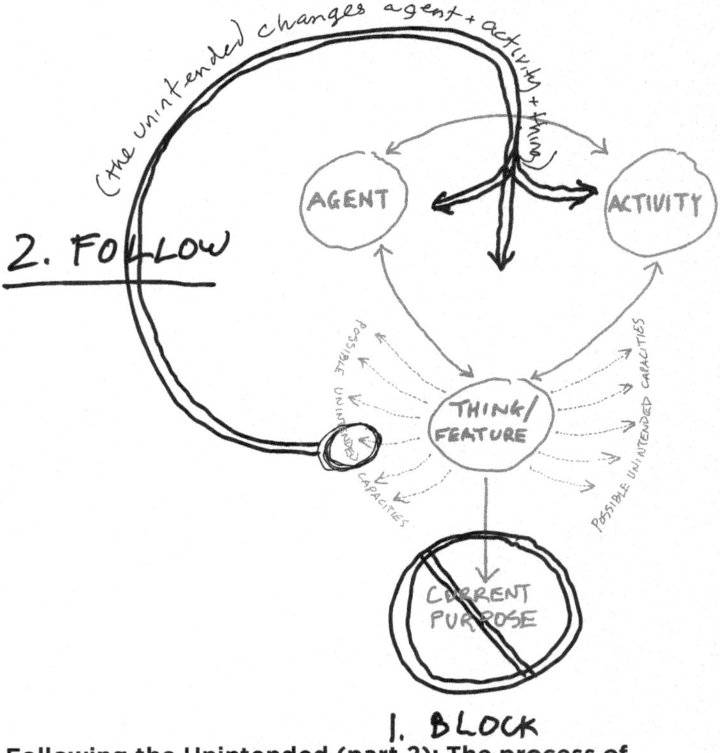

(the unintended changes agent + activity + thing)
2. FOLLOW
AGENT
ACTIVITY
THING/
FEATURE
POSSIBLE UNINTENDED CAPACITIES
POSSIBLE UNINTENDED CAPACITIES
CURRENT
PURPOSE
1. BLOCK

Following the Unintended (part 2): The process of blocking and following (above)

Why did cartilage first evolve?

One might think it is obvious: to give fish structure. But, that is not the reason — in fact, that is the unintended outcome of what happened: cartilage first evolves to help sequester toxins that could not be effectively flushed out of early oceanic beings.

So, now fish have bones that unintentionally help them swim — what next?

Not so fast. The cartilage goes through various twists and turns to get to this point — essentially a series of these sideways movements of purpose being pushed aside by the unintended being discovered in action. There is no linear path here. Just a lot of branchings and many twists and turns.

But, we can skip ahead to fins?

Sure, by chance fins evolved in two directions: one type joined the body in a single spot (lobe finned), while most joined the body at more points (ray finned).

Mutations diversified these designs and the variations allowed form unintended possibilities to emerge.

Many of these minor mutations of a lobe fin developed appendages that we would now recognize as "legs"

So the ocean was full of "legged" fish swimming around?

Sure, and it still is. Each of these leg-fins affords certain beneficial actions and each harbors unintended capacities.

It is not just about the fins right? Wouldn't you need lungs to breathe on land? A flatter body perhaps and eyes looking in the right direction?

Yes. Many other changes were going on in parallel.

Lungs surprisingly evolved quite early on and many early fish had both lungs and gills. It is believed that lungs are an unintended by-product of digestive "cough" reflex in primitive fish. In most fish lungs evolved into swim bladders because lungs were not necessary but had the unintended capacity to regulate buoyancy.

And fish bodies definitely varied and some larger fish developed longer slender bodies suited to stalking in underwater seaweed beds and tall underwater grasses.

Eyes moved towards the top of the head to help some fish eat airborne creatures like flies.

So we have many converging lines of unintended capacities?

Yes, and each of these lines consists of a long series of mutations making intended features and unintended features — and all of these features are being activated in novel ways over and over again.

And at some point land comes into play?

Well, yes — there was a leg-finned fish who enjoyed hunting in shallower plant-filled waters where their leg-fins gave them the advantage of both pushing off the bottom to ambush other fish and allowed them to stealthily swim through the grasses by gently pushing them aside with their leg-fins. They were quite big — over a meter but their young would regularly, perhaps at first accidentally find themselves on land in an attempt to escape being eaten. Now their leg-fins, lungs, arms, long bodies, etc. unintentionally afforded them new possibilities. Which at first must have been very modest — the ability for a few of them to push themselves back into the water when the chase was over. But eventually, a new feedback loop evolves between unintended capacities, their further mutations, new behaviors, and an environment that allows them to live on land. At this "moment" it would be right to say that a wholly new "world" emerges — the world of land animals.

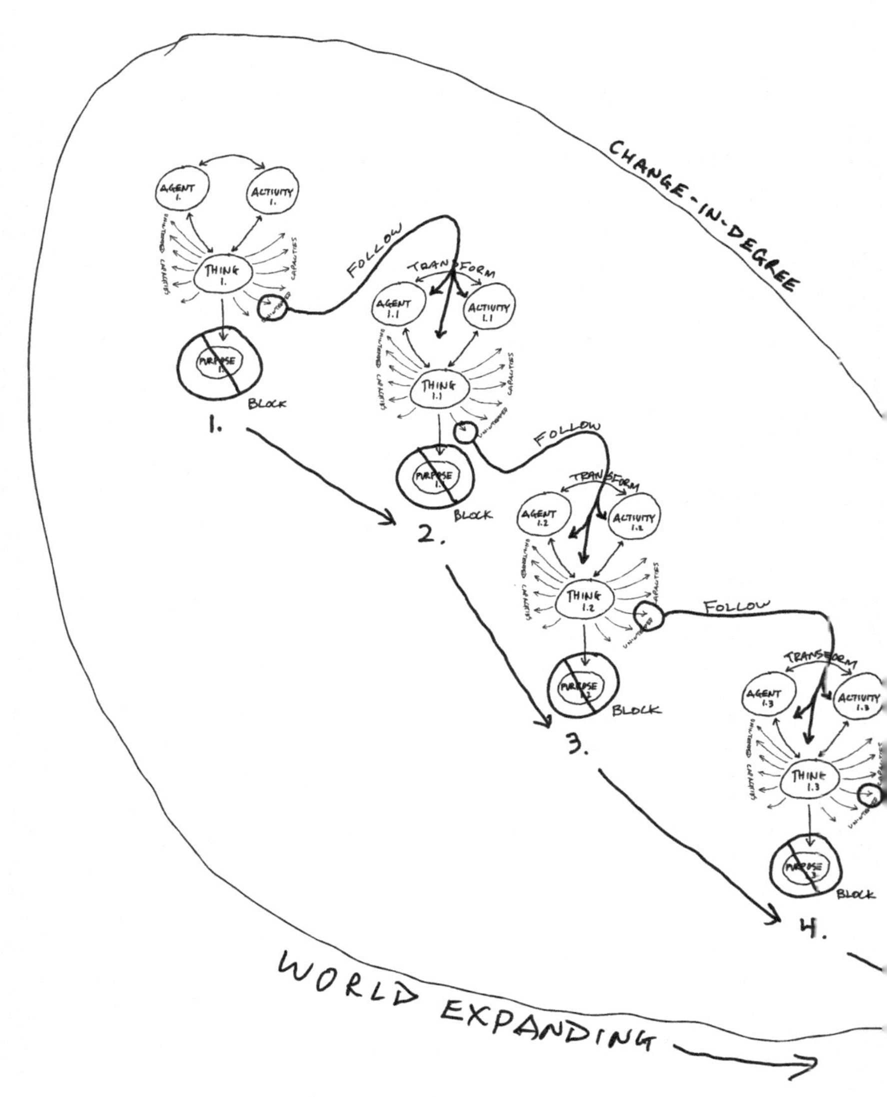
CHANGE-IN-DEGREE
AGENT 1.
ACTIVITY 1.
THING 1.
PURPOSE 1.
BLOCK
1.
FOLLOW
TRANSFORM
AGENT 1.1
ACTIVITY 1.1
THING 1.1
CAPACITIES
PURPOSE 1.1
BLOCK
2.
FOLLOW
TRANSFORM
AGENT 1.2
ACTIVITY 1.2
THING 1.2
PURPOSE 1.2
BLOCK
3.
FOLLOW
TRANSFORM
AGENT 1.3
ACTIVITY 1.3
THING 1.3
PURPOSE
BLOCK
4.
WORLD EXPANDING

So this is the process we could use for a new approach to innovation?

Yes, the sideways step-by-step process of detournement until a threshold is crossed from a change in degree to a change in kind. And then developing this novel world.

Is there a type of "blocking" going on in this process?

That's a critical part of all of this: Essentially at each step of the process the major purpose or affordance of a feature is ignored, or "blocked" as you put it — and a process is undertaken to discover what else it can do. This process of ignoring is a type of blocking or creative negation.

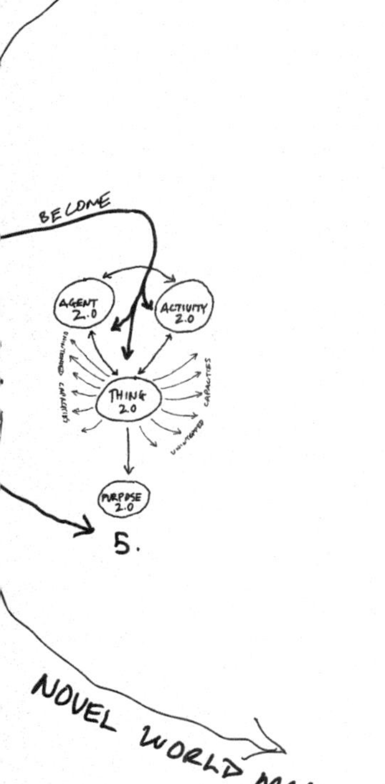

So this is what people mean when they say "break all the rules"?

Sure, it's a bit like that. You're experimentally breaking the "rules" for how something is used. *But, just as importantly you are making new rules.*

This new understanding of the process of evolution is of major importance to reinventing creativity and putting it on a surer footing. The process of evolutionary change — evolutionary invention really is at its core an emergent "purpose switching" of features via unintended capacities to entirely novel ways of being alive (from water life to land life).

In evolutionary theory, this process of utilizing unintended capacities is termed "exaptation". The term means "outside of aptation". Aptation meaning a feature that suits an organism to its environment. Exaptation is in contrast "adaptation" which is the further development of a characteristic to suit a creature to its existing environment.

Exaptation and Adaptation mirror the logic of change-in-kind and change-in-degree.

We can thus conceptualize the process of innovation as being composed of two distinct design logics: Exaptive Design and Adaptive Design. Exaptive Design is used to develop disruptive novelty, and Adaptive Design is used to improve something.

exaptations and affordances

We need to go down a seeming wormhole for a moment: what do we mean by "features"? An eye or a foot is a feature. A cup handle or a chair seat are also features. It is easy to think of these things as fixed, obvious, and objective.

But this is not the case. The cup handle is only a "handle" if you have a hand. It is of critical importance to innovation to keep in mind that *the features of things or creatures that we are talking about are not neutral, obvious or objective.*

Features only show up as what they "are" in action. (This connects back to our Crow — things or in this case features are what they can do in a certain context for a certain subject (the crow for example).

Features are relational.

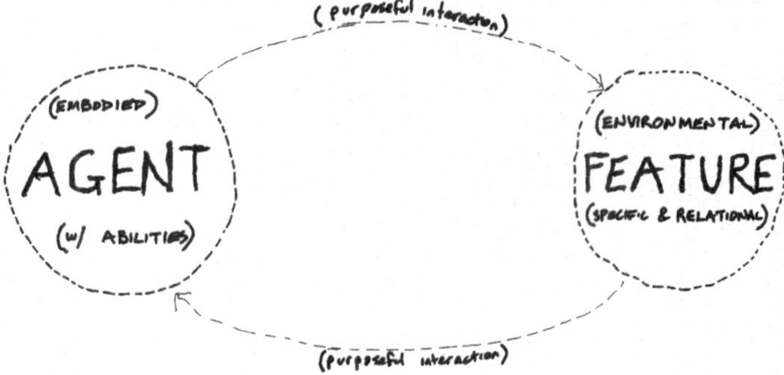

You cannot "see" them by being a disinterested neutral observer of reality — they only emerge in action or when following action (use).

A thing is its use. A feature is its use. A chair "seat" only exists for those who could sit in it — no spider or crow thinks of a chair as being a tool for sitting. Chairs don't show up for spiders or crows.

In regards to creativity, a better way to talk about features is with the term "affordances." This term, from ecological psychology, focuses on what the feature affords or allows (for a specific creature in a specific context). Thus a feature/affordance is best thought of as a directly sensed "opportunity for potential action".

Think of how often in the course of the day we use whatever is handy to do things: we step on a chair to change a bulb, or a dishcloth to grab a hot pan, or a large mug as a smartphone speaker. In these moments we see the world around us directly for what it *affords.*

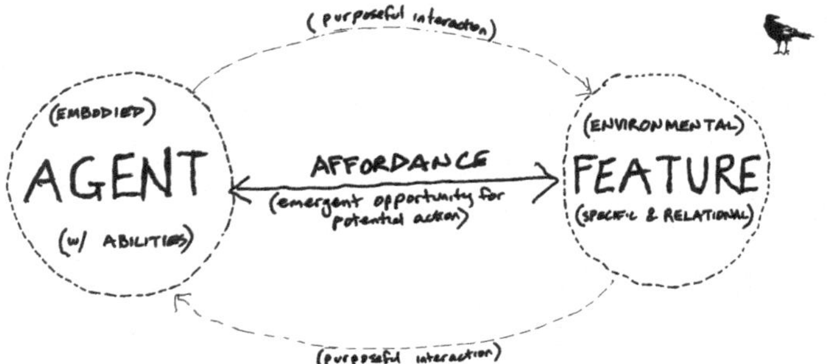

Drawing upon what we just learned from evolutionary theory we can understand the world being composed of two types of affordances for any situated creature (an inventor for example): intentional affordances and unintentional affordances. And the process of innovation as involving the experimental ability to block one, and experimentally draw the other into existence:

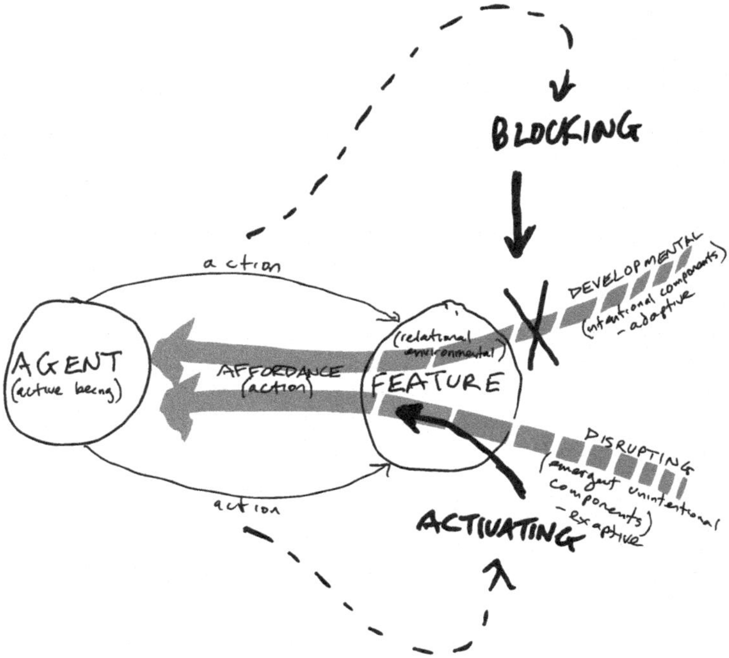

what of human innovation?

Exaptations are not limited to biological evolution; we see them in *all* innovations from GPS to the internet, to antibiotics. What is critical is:

1. This emergence of novelty from the unintended is an iterative process — one unintended possibility leading to another unintended possibility to another in a series of sideways moves and unanticipatedly leaps;
2. As such — there is no "creator" in the literal sense of the word, only a someone or some group that is experimental and attentive to a difference that might be important at the initial stages of creation. The interactions and the total agency of the system are critical. We collaboratively notice, foster, follow, nourish and stabilize...
3. Creativity and innovation happen in sensing, following and allowing oneself to be transformed by the unintended, such that novelty can emerge.
4. At some point, a threshold is crossed and a novel way of being alive emerges (a new world emerges). And this is what we are looking for when we pursue disruptive innovation: worldmaking.

Things both have a purpose and exceed their given purpose. And we as designers can improve the given purpose (developmental design, or adaptive design), or we could experiment towards radical novelty by ignoring, refusing or even *blocking* the given purpose as we follow unintended possibilities (disruptive design, or exaptive design).

To gain skill in exaptive design it is important to understand all the forms of exaptivity:

1. *Intentional Components with unintended but existing effects:* This is the form we come across most often. When we use a chair as a ladder, or a shoe as a wine bottle opener we are using an intentional feature for an unintended but existing purpose. Ladders and bottle openers exist. In this

way, we are not inventing a new purpose. Most often when we do this we are really developing an existing thing or purpose. But, in experimenting with things in this way we can often see a way it could leap outside of its current category of use.

2. *Intentional Components that no longer have a use:* A great example of this is HipHop using the turntable and record in new ways as a true musical instrument which led to the emergence of a new way of being alive. Blocking intention is a good way to artificially catalyze this process: what else can something do if we ignore its purpose? The modern tattoo machine is another example — it was an electric pen that no one wanted.
3. *Unintentional Components that are physical by-products:* In every physical object there are parts that directly contribute to the purpose and there are parts that are there simply as necessary by-products: The extra skin under a squirrel arm that could afford it the ability to glide. Or the classical example from architecture: the spandrel — it is a novel feature that comes about when you connect a dome to four columns. This is perhaps the richest resource for exaptive design.
4. *Unintentional Components that are chance by-products:* We find these often in nature: a random mutation that has no impact, but later is activated to do something entirely novel. Usually only noticed in activity. The use of the drip in painting by Jackson Pollock and others is a good example. A variation of this is accidents and failures. Sticky Notes — the glue that did not stick...
5. *Unintentional Components working in category:* Most often these novel unintended uses stay within their category (Pollock is still painting). This should not be seen as limiting their innovation: Pollock was filmed dripping paint onto canvases in a dancelike manner, which unintentionally led other artists to experiment with art as "action + chance" which developed into an alternative paradigm for art.

6. *Unintentional Components working across category:* Hummingbird feathers and flight being used to make bird calls: the unintended use leaves the category of movement and enters or develops a whole new category of expression. The Wright brothers using hip steering in bikes to develop steering in gliders. These potential world-making leaps are of critical importance to innovation.

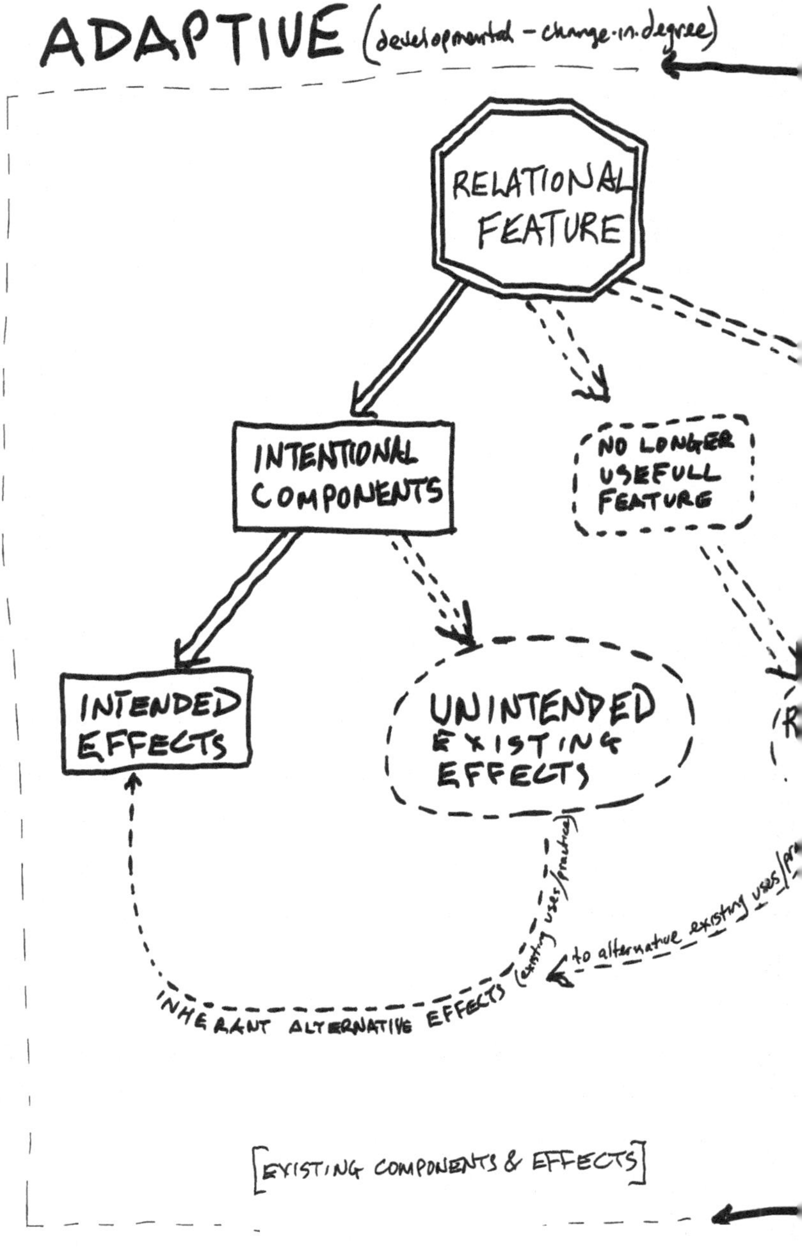

ADAPTIVE (developmental – change-in-degree)

RELATIONAL FEATURE

INTENTIONAL COMPONENTS

NO LONGER USEFULL FEATURE

INTENDED EFFECTS

UNINTENDED EXISTING EFFECTS

R

INHERANT ALTERNATIVE EFFECTS (existing uses/practices)

to alternative existing uses/pr

[EXISTING COMPONENTS & EFFECTS]

EXAPTIVE (disruptive change-in-kind)

UNINTENTIONAL COMPONENTS

SING

NECESSARY PHYSICAL BY-PRODUCT

CHANCE PHYSICAL BY-PRODUCT (invisible introduction)

IN CATEGORY EFFECT

OUTSIDE CATEGORY EFFECT "injections"

[NOVEL COMPONENTS & EFFECTS]

affordance and exaptation are critical, but...

The hard thing with developing a new framework for innovation is that there are so many equally critical concepts and each informs and transforms the others. We need to understand all of them — and all of them at the same time!

While understanding both affordances and exaptation goes a long way — it is easy to misunderstand these concepts. The big mistake is to imagine that affordances and exaptations are pre-existing things "out there" that just need to be discovered.

As innovators, a red flag needs to go off every time we hear the word *discovery*. If the genuinely new does not pre-exist (if it did it would not be the new) — then there is never anything "out there" quietly awaiting discovery.

the new emerges from the middle of "nothing"

Back to our paradoxes: the new cannot exist prior to it existing. It is not hidden waiting to be discovered. It is nowhere. It does not exist. So "where" is it?

Everything has to come from somewhere — unless it is a true miracle — but then we are no longer talking about what humans can do or science can explain.

Here is the paradox: From where does the new arise if it must arise from somewhere but that somewhere cannot already exist as the new?

(Just know, this hurts us too — paradoxes are painful.)

the something from nothing paradox:

Put simply: how can we go from nothing to something?

The "something from nothing" paradox is intimately linked to the Innovation Paradox. As we discussed the ancient Greeks struggled deeply with how "something could come from nothing" and proposed the metaphysical answer that we in the West have relied upon ever since:

You can't really get something from nothing — there has to be a fixed beginning from which everything else emerges: reductionism. For something novel to concur, there has to already be something in some other realm or hidden inside things themselves that has always been there and that all creation follows (a pre-established plan).

This model has shaped the Western mindset for over 2000+ years. It is a mindset and model that has made us look everywhere for either a being that has pre-planned everything or for a hidden pre-existing plan inside each and every being. In a nutshell: Essentialism + Reductionism.

It is the mindset that meant creativity in the modern sense did not exist in western thought as a concept until the 1800's.

But this ancient metaphysical answer to the "something from nothing" paradox simply begs the question: *Then who made that being or original plan?*

We end up with the infinite regression that children are so fond of:

And who made God?

And who made that being before God?

And what was before that?

And on and on...

But, it turns out there is no need to begin with a pre-established plan or a pre-given essence to answer the paradox of something from nothing: we now know that order can spontaneously emerge from chaos, and that the new can *"emerge"* from existing systems while being irreducible to them. This concept of emergence has now been well studied by the field of complexity science.

EMERGENCE:

Emergence in this technical sense of the term means that the novel property that "emerges" is:

1. Greater and distinct from the sum of the parts that made it, while also being:
2. Irreducible to these parts, and
3. Exhibit a relational holism
4. Emergent novelty can make its own parts (global to local influence).
5. Emergent properties are instantiations of an Emergent Process.

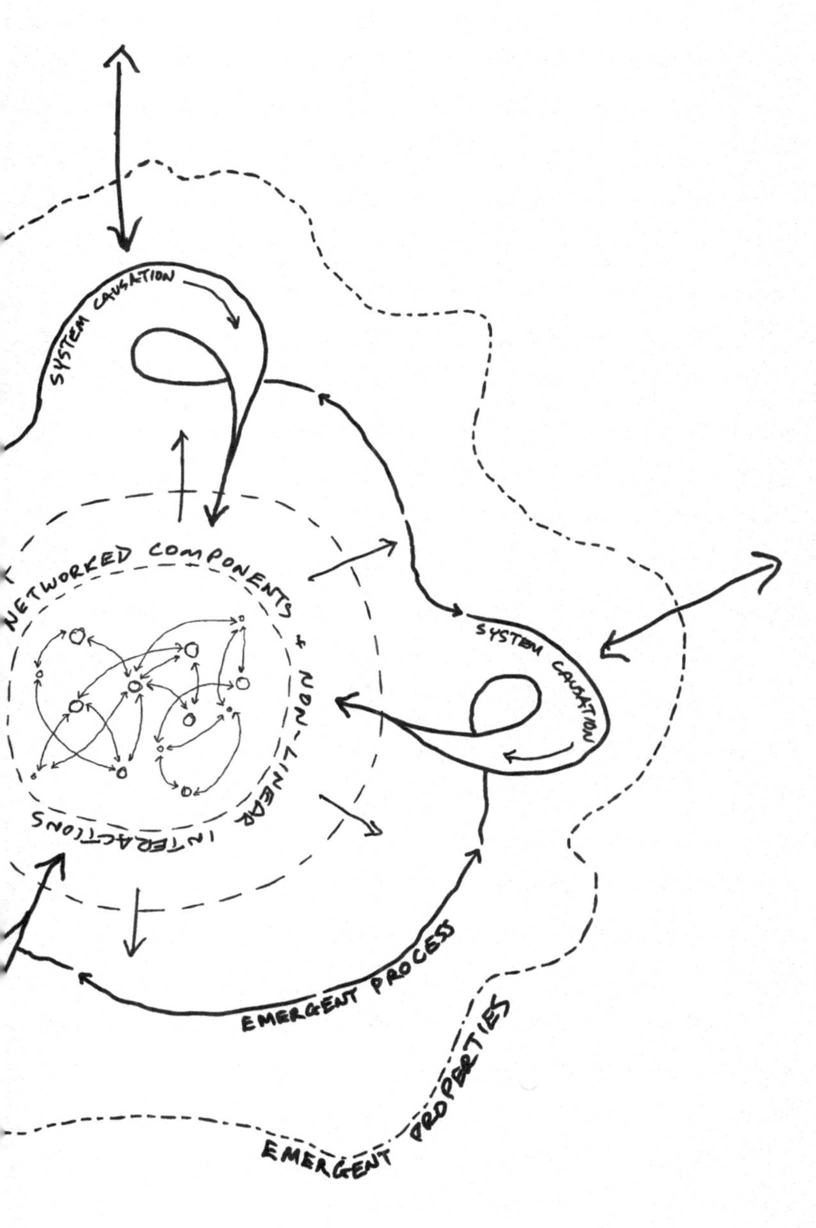

SYSTEM CAUSATION
NETWORKED COMPONENTS
+ NON-LINEAR INTERACTIONS
SYSTEM CAUSATION
EMERGENT PROCESS
EMERGENT PROPERTIES

This concept of emergence is an *ontological* one, for it argues that this feature of irreducibility to being explained by components parts is not simply because of a lack of current knowledge about how things really work — but that there is actually something real, new and distinct that has emerged which is irreducible to its component parts.

Emergence is an example of a complex non-linear process that is non-decomposable, with many levels of feedback and operating in a semi-autonomous manner. A key aspect of emergent processes is that they are *irreducibly relational*. Evan Thompson describes emergent features in this way: "They are constituted by relations that are not exhaustively determined by or reducible to the intrinsic properties of the elements so related. These holistic relations do not simply influence the parts, but supersede or subsume their independent existence in an irreducibly relational structure".

There are many examples of emergence all around us -- that we are conscious beings -- is a classical example of emergence.

Consciousness is something that requires having a brain, but is irreducible to the brain, and it changes the brain.

Cultural phenomena are equally emergent — coming out of the relational totality of bodies, practices, implicit sensibilities, tools, environments and shared histories.

Why does this matter for creativity? We so often understand making as a process of addition. We add parts together and get a whole (Think of how we assembled things with Lego as a child). Here the parts make the whole and the whole can be taken back apart and each part can be analyzed to understand the whole. This is a reductive model of making.
We can reduce the final product to the parts and the process. Cars can be built this way on a production line.

But the genuinely new does not come about in this additive and subtractive linear manner. Disruptive innovations — changes in kind are best thought of as types of dynamic co-emergent processes that harness and activate chaotic processes iteratively via techniques of blocking.

Here it is important to remember that chaos — actual chaos, is not a totally random phenomenon. Chaos is always tending towards and dissipating from brief moments of spontaneous novel order. This can be both activated and stabilized. This is what we see happening both in evolution (the fin to foot) and the development of new art movements (the drip to new paradigms of art).

Open engagement and the unintentional *interaction* of things spontaneously generate higher-level order. Interactions — relations between things, self-organize into semi-stable states. Our practices of making interact with these ongoing processes of the creative universe, transforming itself such that "our" innovations and creativity are systems level emergences.

At this point, we can bring back the concept that exaptive features are forms of radical novel affordances. Affordances are activity dependent relations between an agent and its environment that are irreducible to any fixed property of the environment. Exaptive affordances are the unintended relation potentials that only exist in their realization. Which is to say exaptive affordances spring into being as potential pathways for novelty via an emergent process. Exaptations are genuinely novel, context-dependent, and relational. Evolutionary exaptations in natural history are contingent — if you rewound the clock back to the period prior to fish coming onto land and then let evolution play out again — something totally different and equally radical novel could have emerged and we would never have come into being.

creativity is emergent

One cannot understand the universe or creativity reductively. To say that "novelty emerges" is to say something very particular. Emergence is dependent upon but irreducible to its component parts. Novelty emerges in a way that exceeds what preceded it. As such, creativity absolutely exceeds the known. We mean this in a fundamental sense, the pre-stateable laws and conditions of a situation are exceeded by the emergence of novelty. *Novelty cannot be known in advance.* Working with creativity means to work with the non-knowable (not simply because we are not smart enough or don't have a powerful enough computer, they are simply futures that are *not* knowable in advance). This universe is a spontaneously emergent self-organizing universe. Creativity is part of this emergence. The theoretical biologist Stewart Kaufmann says it well, "How can we not be stunned by the fact that the biosphere... and human cultural evolution are co-constructing wholes despite partial lawlessness? We are indeed, beyond the Galilean spell, into creativity and emergence, to the unknown mystery into which we must all live our lives."

This radically curtails the classical ways we work (via techniques of decomposition, getting to the essence, returning to the origin and gaining oversight). Things, while decomposable, are emergent wholes in which their parts exist because of and for the whole. All of our classical techniques work reasonably well to deal with closed systems and simple forms of causality — the probables of our lives — but not the possibles — the strange emergent novelties that are so disruptive. Emergence means that you cannot start at the end (with something like a version of your final idea) to be creative. All of our techniques of solution-driven design utilizing brainstorming and ideation miss this critical truth.

Reality is open, complex, non-linear, entangled, systemic, ongoing — and so are the most vexing issues we face today.

Today we so often as makers continue to assume a closed world of discreet things and problems that is ruled by simple forms of causality. It is the failures and limits of these classical ideas and techniques that have played a significant role in our current ecological crisis. A major goal of this text is to move us towards more resilient ethical models of ecological emergent co-making, this requires a fundamental shift in our thinking and practices and broader cultural mindset. This approach requires us to be a lot more humble, collaborative, experimental, embedded, and long-term than we are used to as contemporary makers.

we are blind and thoughtless in the face of the new:

If the radically new is exaptive and emergent it is nowhere till it begins to happen. Because of this foresight, prediction, trend analysis, and deep knowledge of the past will not be of any direct help. Radical novelty is ontologically new.

It is a truly shocking surprise.

Of course, it might make sense and be explainable in retrospect, but that does not help one in the middle of co-emerging with the new.

If we are blind and thinking is of little help — what's left? *How do we work?*

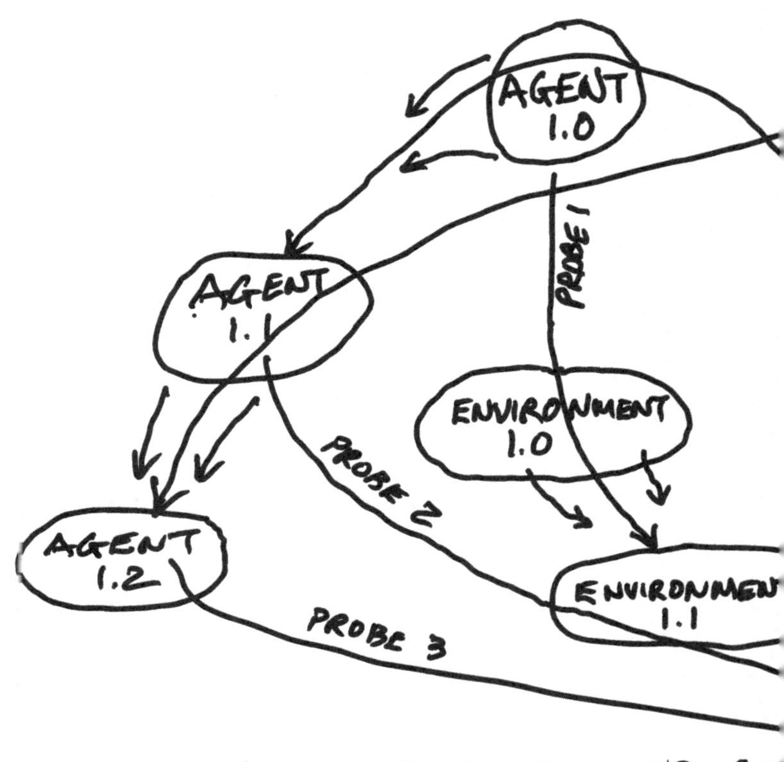

1. creativity happens when all action is probing

Reality, when looked at from the perspective of creativity, is simply too chaotic, dynamic, relational and emergent to gain a clear summative understanding.. If you try and pause things, and analytically pull it apart and understand the pieces all you will have is a narrow understanding of the pieces — but not the distinct but connected dynamic and emergent whole. Knowing root causes and developing predictive models will not work. So what can we do?

Probe.

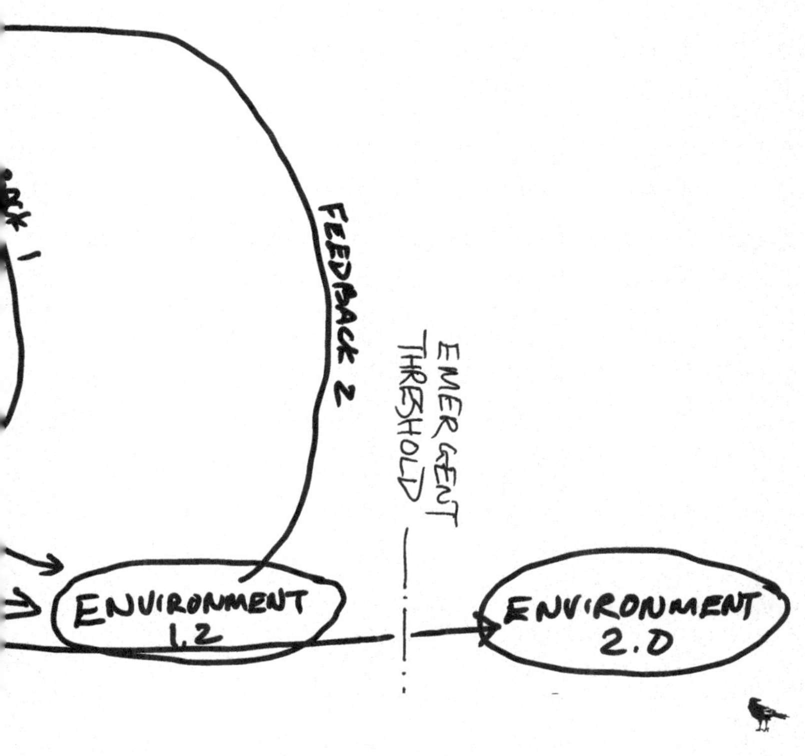

Highly dynamic systems cannot be "understood" but we can perturbate them in specific experimental ways. The system will respond, and then we can adjust (both ourselves, our tools and our environment) and probe again. In this way, we are "making a path in walking it." We are attuning and transforming ourselves to make ever move successful novel assemblages emerge via a series of iterative probes and feedback/feedforward loops. This active probing involves developing exaptive tests (blocking & following). Like the fish, we will co-emerge with a new world (we, and our transformation, are never outside of the process).

2. if it cannot be thought, how does one think it?

Creativity is non-conceptualizable in its beginnings.

So, how does one conceptualize the

non-conceptualizable?

We are always coming back to this: thinking is involved, we clearly cannot dismiss it entirely from the innovation process. But, we also know that the pathway to radical novelty cannot be centered on ideation (happening in the head/brain).

The way out of this paradox is not to develop better thinking techniques or mental exercises to make the mind more creative. The answer is strikingly simple: we can quite easily sidestep the paradox by realizing that creativity is the outcome of practices: *before we have an idea we are already doing something or making something or engaged in something novel that we cannot explain* and ultimately at this stage do not need to explain (if we could).

Before developing this, we need to reflect on the role thinking does and does not play in our everyday lives. You reach for your cup of coffee or walk across the room and sit down. You do not need to think through and plan out your every action and muscle movement. You reach for and drink from your coffee cup without much thought, just as you make it across the room and fall onto the sofa without any real thought.

Much of our lives involves a tacit "know-how" — we do things — without requiring much — or even any "know-what" (complex thinking, knowing and planning). Many of the most skillful things we do — say rolling a kayak or breastfeeding are not things we could even put into words and explain without great effort. Often when we try to think about or articulate what we do in these nuanced practices we lose our way.

Thinking — knowing what — subsists upon and arises out of a far broader world of embodied and engaged know-how. The foundations of our lives, practices, values, and sense of being are ultimately unconceptualizable — it rests and thrives in action. Changing diapers, holding hands, serving dinner, watering plants, worrying when you see a police officer all ground our lives in ways that exceed ideation.

innovation and tacit behavior

Engaged forms of play, puttering, tinkering, improvising, messing about, open experimentation, intentional stupidity, or curious observation while using novel tools in novel situations — are all common examples of how we sidestep the innovation paradox.

These are all examples of active open-ended experimental practices of *making and doing: probing*. Now what is critical in these practices is that we are doing two things: (1) making in a hands-on manner (at any scale), and (2) attending to the emergence of novel bodily sensations (affect) — feeling that something interesting, odd or curious is happening. This mix of open experimentation (doing) plus attending to differences that arise alongside vague *feelings* is a critical part of the beginning of the journey to making-discovering the new. Remember this is not the "kernel" of an idea -- the fish is feeling this directly as an embodied affect — and so too is a community.

At this delicate early moment of early doing-sensing, novelty can easily slip away, for it is not something we can recognize -- it is too new for that — in fact, we most often misrecognize it as a mistake — an error to be corrected. The mindset of play, tinkering, puttering, and probing are helpful precisely because they do not seek to overly conceptualize or judge. It is the rush to ideate that derails the early phase of the creative process.

As we openly experiment these feelings of difference are followed and our experiment takes on a heading as a feeling evolves into vague hunches arising through the force of the experiment itself (wayfinding). In activity, skills emerge alongside vague hunches, which lead one to follow a direction that slowly develops via intuitions, and swerving experiments into novel practices that only much, later on, are fully conceptualized as a new "idea".

Most of our lives are lived in this space of vague sensing and direct action. Clear and specific thought is a much smaller part of our daily lives than we imagine.

Emergent Wayfinding for Creativity

We can break down this process of emergent wayfinding into discrete steps for the sake of analysis (in reality they are far more mixed and continuously feedback/feedforward into each other). There are two phases:

1. Embodied Doing
2. Embodied Knowing

In the first phase knowing is implicit and tacit — the knowledge is non-articulable but exists directly in the emerging habits, practices and embodied skills, and vague feelings. Humberto Manturana terms this *"knowing-how without knowing-what"*. In the second phase these tacit forms of knowing slowly become articulable and eventually turn into abstractions that can stand on their own as fully-fledged concepts.

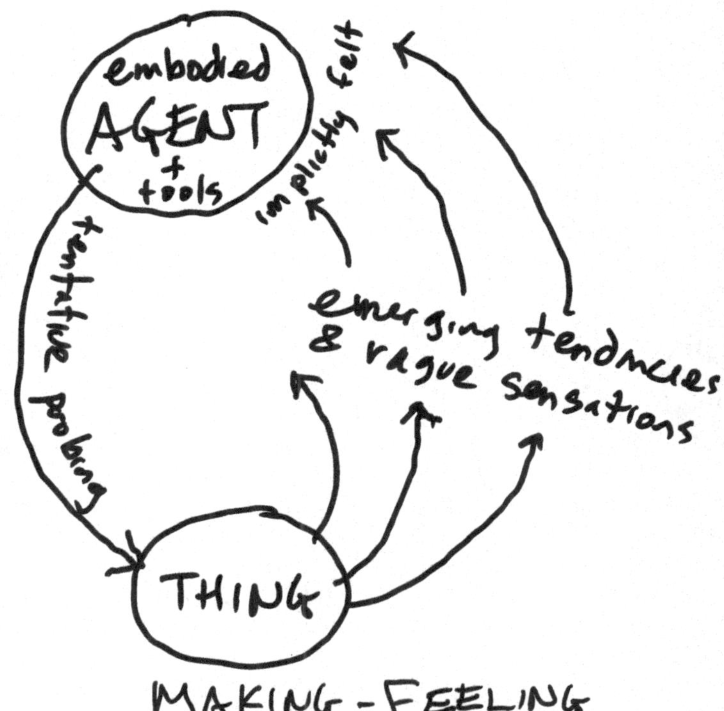

emergent wayfinding for creativity:

PHASE ONE: EMBODIED DOING

(Know-how, Tacit ecologically distributed & emergent embodied abilities, open experimentation)

1. making-feeling: sensing through making:

Experimental doing-with (novel tools, environments and skills) and letting sensing-feeling tendencies vaguely co-emerge from *within* objects-in-the-making and return into the process. Joining resonances and tuning rhythms at an embodied/environmental level. Events arise and are stabilized when possible — these both take time and emerge as new forms of time. Vague sensations of "Interesting" and "puzzling" tendencies and events are felt and might rise to an intuitive level of attention. *Change is lived, but not represented.* Empathy.

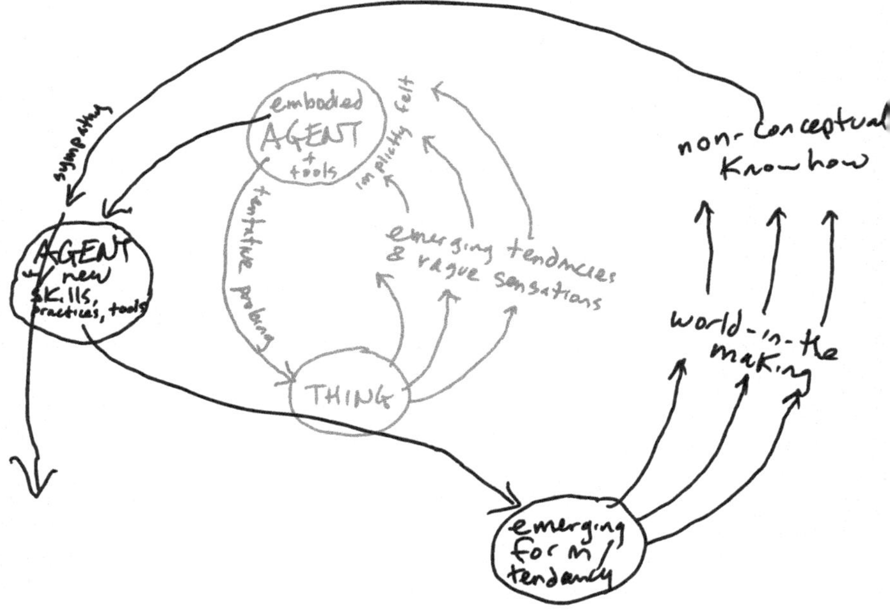

MAKING-DIALOGING

2. making-dialoging: thinking with making:

Active following of an emerging form/tendency and responding (in the experiment): making-thinking with the emerging quasi-object crossing one or many thresholds (of capacity and stability). Signs act as triggers. Embodied skills, tools and practices co-develop in a back & forth between things and actions. Matter/things co-evolve forms immanent to the process. Non-conceptual know-how co-emerges with a "world-in-the-making" (concrete skills for repetition, expansion and discovery). We are living with things (as opposed to knowing things abstractly). Sympathy.

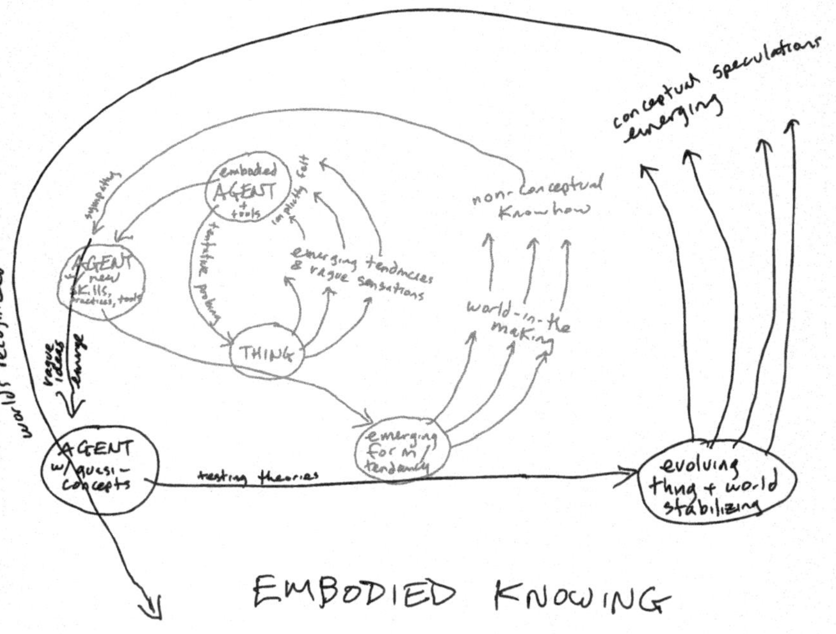

PHASE TWO: EMBODIED KNOWING

(Know-what, abstract conceptual knowledge, ideation of invention-discovery)

3. thinking-making: making with thinking:

A vague idea about the thing/action (what is it?) emerges and flows back into the making-using-developing process. Quasi-concepts become useful & are tested, stabilized & reactivated. Nascent "theories" are proposed & put to work/tested.

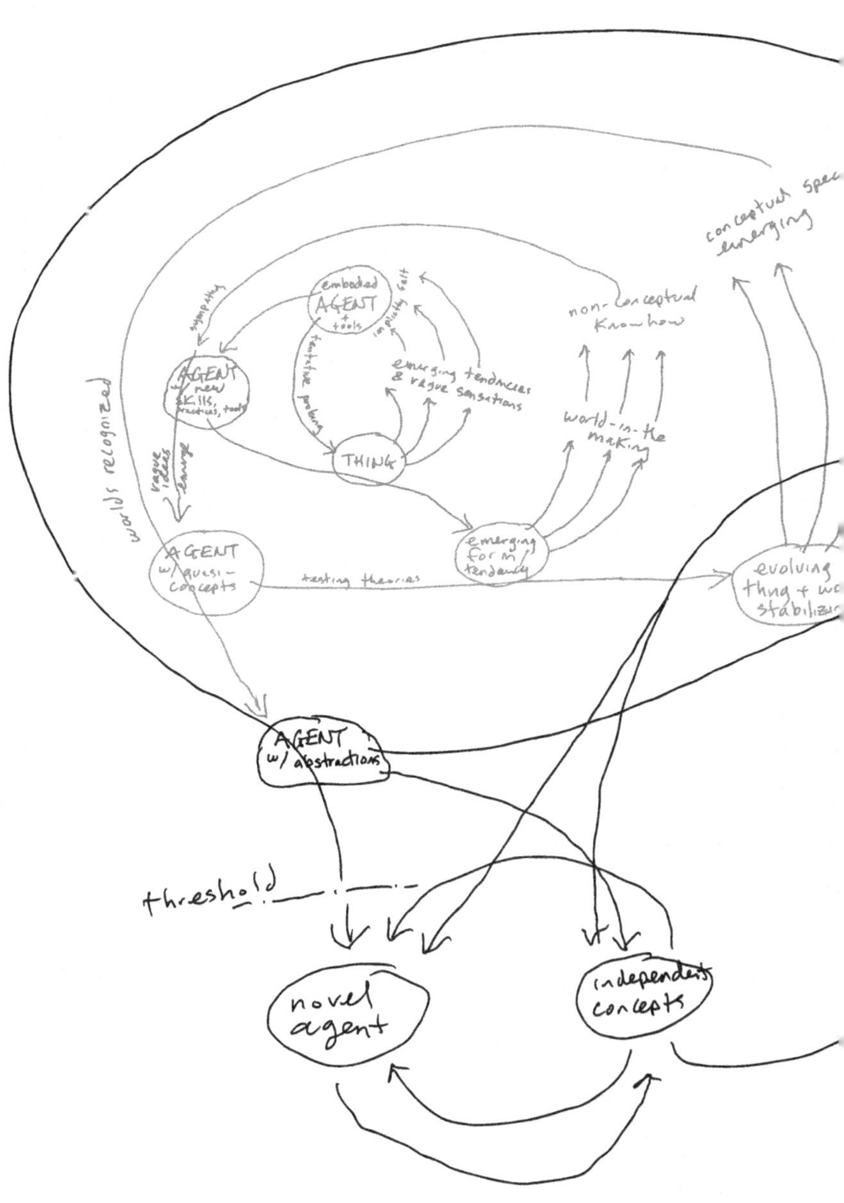

conceptual spec
emerging
embodied AGENT + tools
non-conceptual know-how
sympathy
implicitly felt
tentative probing
AGENT new skills, practices, tools
emerging tendencies & vague sensations
world-in-the making
worlds recognized
vague ideas
THING
AGENT w/ quasi-concepts
emerging form/tendency
testing theories
evolving thing + wo stabilizi
AGENT w/ abstractions
threshold
novel agent
independent concepts

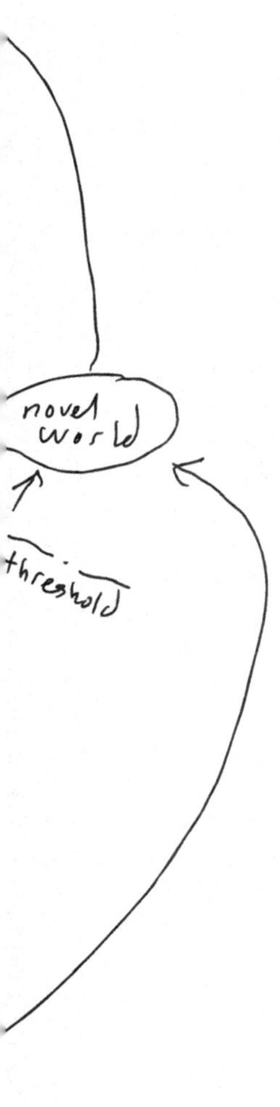

4. thinking-thinking: thinking about thinking after making:

Abstraction of concepts from objects/ practices. These abstractions feedback (know-how) and feedforward (theories, paradigms, approaches, modes of being) into new iterations of the process. Abstraction.

For our purposes what matters here can be summed up thus: *creativity is not a "thing" that some, or all of us, possess — it is a worldly ecological practice in which any of us can participate*.

Thus creativity, like any other phenomenon that we might imagine happening in the mind/brain, is a dynamic, multi-centered, embedded worldly phenomenon/activity. For too long we have divorced thinking from making, but to avoid the Innovation Paradox and allow for novel innovations to arise we need to realize that making is thinking, and doing precedes conceptualization, and this all happens in a robust highly networked environment.

creativity is an aberrant beauty

What makes a novel world hold together and become visible to us despite its newness?

This is a challenging question: if a novel world is qualitatively different and the criteria, logics, process, and values of the previous world do not hold — how will we ever recognize a new world as it first begins to tentatively emerge? Newness, as we know from our previous discussion of tacit knowledge, is first *felt* prior to being fully conceptualized.

Broad, pervasive and overall sensations (moods or feelings) are part of all experience. In everyday life, while doing mundane tasks, we are accompanied by a pervasive sense of contentment, peace, ease, recognition, and perhaps a little boredom (frustration). And equally, when we move away from the known into difference and novelty distinct qualitative sensations arise and can cue us into the fact that we are onto something different and perhaps important: As our experiments lead us into more chaotic and uncharted territories we feel either "nothing" (this is that feeling of frustration/boredom that sometimes accompanies things that are different: when we experience the odd, but we are impatient because they are not what we recognize, expect or instinctively want) or a form of perplexity. This feeling of perplexity can either be discomforting and subtly push us back into the known, or this perplexity and discomfort can come to feel like a force that propels us further into following an experiment. Then as an experiment evolves towards a nascent world where we are accompanied by a sensation of something like wonder or wonder-horror (wow, but where is this taking us?), or even wonder-disgust (wow, but I would never do that). Then as a novel world fully co-emerges with us, it evokes in us a sense of beauty. Now it will not be a beauty we recognize or feel comfortable with — it will be a feeling of an *aberrant beauty* a — novel and altogether strange, but nonetheless compelling, beauty — a disconcerting beauty.

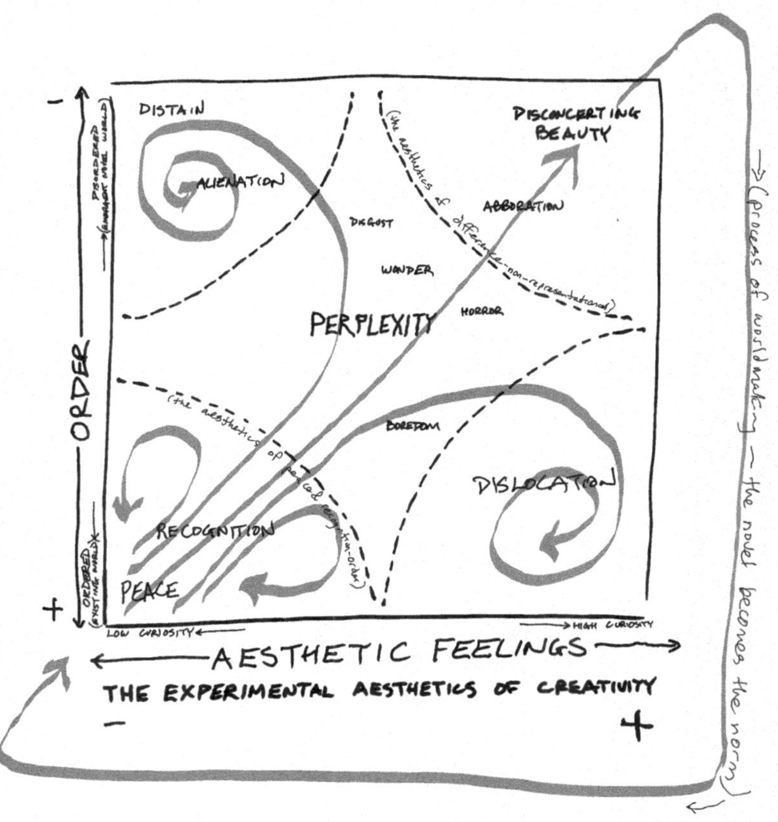

Beauty in general is how we sense a world *as a world* — that it is something bigger than we can see, sense, or know *and that it holds together* — we feel it as a beautiful world. Sensing, and welcoming, disconcerting forms of beauty is a critically important skill — it cues us into the opening up of newness in its nascent state. Additionally welcoming these feelings of perplexity, bewilderment, horror, disgust, boredom and wonder open us to an encounter with difference (a new piece of music, a strange cultural artifact, or experiencing a new activity). These feelings are aesthetic feelings -- sensations of beauty. The sensations of beauty and the aesthetic dimensions of experience (and their cultivation) are critical to creativity and invention.

A new form of beauty is integral to a new world — for a novel world gives us new ways to sense, feel, do, see, and think — which is aesthetics. This feeling and new modes of sensing of wonder and beauty become slowly conceptualizable and enter into discourse and debate and thus transforms into new values, and truths. *Beauty precedes and exceeds truth* as novelty emerges. What is the making of beauty? It is a composition of non-conceptual feelings entangling with the unintended in a strange relay towards a difference that makes a difference. But will this be the beauty we know? No. The new is an aberrant strange and acquired beauty. It beckons us further, it pulls us out and draws us in -- we sense something other and we follow...

"the only thing that makes life possible is permanent, intolerable uncertainty: not knowing what comes next"

u. k. le guin

PART THREE: STARTING & STAYING IN THE MIDDLE:

With this broad understanding of innovation, emergence, and how to move beyond the innovation paradox, we can now fill in some of the critical contexts for innovation.

ON SYSTEMS, EVENTS, THINGS, AND WORLDS

Life is lived in the middle. The crow finds itself in the midst of an already ongoing situation. It experiments from what it is thrown into. It can never start at some imaginary pure beginning.

The creative life is lived as an interwoven series of ongoing and ultimately unknowable events.

What matters is staying with the middle. Staying with the entangled ongoing relational whole.

When we stop to think about the what and why of things unconsciously we fall into the scripts of our deep cultural habit of pulling everything apart in search of essences.

But where does this desire to get to hidden essences and fundamental building blocks get us?

you can't find anything in anything!

Here's a simple exercise to illustrate the problem: Looking at a bird in flight, where will you find "flight"?

If you pull apart the bird's wings feather by feather will you discover "flight" somewhere inside of something? Is it "in" the feathers? The bones? The Muscles? The shape of the wing?

No, of course not.

Flight is not "in" anything.

Flying is the emergent property of a dynamic system that includes — but is irreducible to — feathers, muscles, gravity, air density, the sun, landscape forms, bones, intentions, practices, ecosystems, evolutionary histories, etc.

Flight happens in the middle.

creativity dwells in the great outdoors

This analogy holds true with creativity: creativity cannot be found "in" any one thing but is the property *of* a system. Creativity also happens in the middle.

It is not in a brain. It is not in a person. It is not in an idea.

Creativity is the emergent property of a *dynamic system* that includes — *but is irreducible to* —bodies, intentions, practices, habits, cultures, ecosystems, material contexts, evolutionary histories, etc.

What matters here is not any one component of the system, but the system itself. It is less about the unique things and more about *how* they relate — their *relationships*. This shift in focus to a systems level is a shift to working at the level that creativity emerges and lives.

Again, not what it is, but what it affords as an integral part of a set of dynamic relations.

It is the whole that produces the properties we so often mistakenly assign to a part of the system. Flight to feathers, creativity to minds. Behavior to genes.

The properties of the whole need to be understood at the level of the whole.

"Events," "Middles" "Assemblages" and "systems" are simply other ways to talk about this contingent dynamic whole.

creativity happens at a systems level

Our practices and habits of inquiry in the contemporary West are to think about reality first and foremost in terms of discreet things. We live in a world of chairs, tables, persons, flowers, birds, mountains, rivers, iPhones...

We have the conceptual habit of breaking things down into component parts and building things back up. Societies are composed of groups, groups are composed of families, families are composed of people, people are composed of cells, cells are composed of molecules, molecules are composed of atoms, and on and on all the way down until we come to a string in eleven dimensional space.

We are always peeling away the layers to get at the final inner ingredient which we then understand as singular and solitary essence. The onion model.

This is connected to its companion habit of neatly

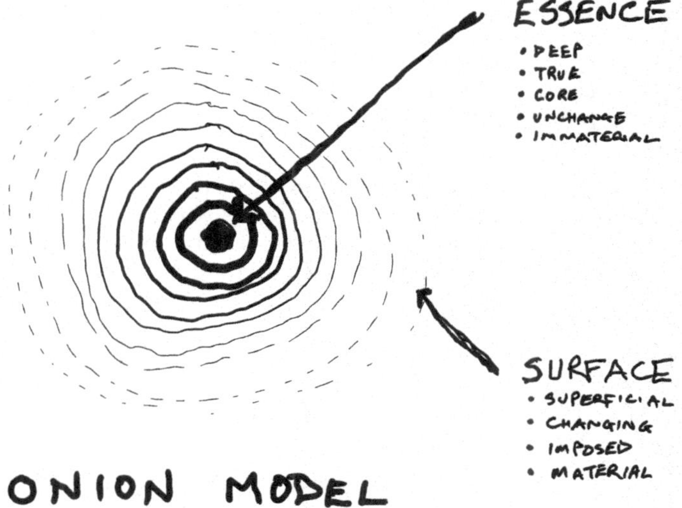

dividing everything into two — essential and superficial. A gesture repeated in all our dualities: with always one term superseding the other as more essential: nature and culture, mind and body, men and women, right and left... But what if the "essence" or logic, or driving force is not in any one thing but held across the whole relationship? What if it is relations all the way down and all the way up?

Perhaps the easiest and first way to understand relations is the connection between things. Love, for example, is not in anything but held between and across people, places, things and activities. Love, creativity, flight, an event or an idea — all of these are things that come from the totality of a set of relations. These "connections" — such as creativity are as real as the things themselves.

Our world is composed of many forms of relationships: feelings, actions, practices, bodies, environments, brains, energy gradients, laws, predetor-prey pairings, concepts, feedback loops, mindsets, and worldviews, are all examples of relationships.

But so too are things -- our hammer, when we grasp and use it is clearly a hard and solid *thing* to us but it is also very much a relational being. A hammer is impossible to imagine without something to hammer. A hammer calls to metals forged into nails and trees sawn into boards and a world where they make sense. This world — this system is one quite distinct from one of vines and woven branches, or mud bricks.

When we see things and all their relationships as connected, we begin to see worlds and systems. But seeing connections is only the beginning. A system is fundamentally more than a set of connected things.

systems are weird

When we connect things, the parts are superseded by the totality and *this totality takes on a logic all of its own* — one that is irreducible to the parts and their initial logics. (Which is why you cannot take systems apart to find out how they work).

Here we are introducing a second concept to the reality of relations — the unique reality of the whole. What is most shocking about systems is that when you put things into a set of relationships something totally new and unexpected will *emerge* (this novelty is what is termed emergence and we will discuss this shortly).

Systems act in unique ways that cannot be understood or *changed* by looking at individual things — in fact considering the parts individually will usually make things worse. This is where understanding systems really matters to creativity and innovation.

Let's dig into a great example: Single-use plastic bags are a serious problem. Many innovators have approached this problem from the perspective that this is an issue that can be addressed by dealing with the plastic bag alone (versus from a systems perspective). This perspective has led to the very popular move to ban plastic bags as a solution. On the surface, it does seem like an ideal solution to curbing the use of plastics and limiting all of the problems that come from these bags and plastic in general. It is a very popular and easy to grasp action: ban bags!

But what actually happens when you ban plastic bags? Does the use of plastics go down? Is the overall harm to the environment reduced? No — the opposite actually happens: the use of plastics and other harmful practices actually goes up. That this might be a surprise, and this surprise is a testament to how poorly we understand systems.

Here is what happens when you ban plastic bags in supermarkets:

1. The first thing to understand is that people use shopping bags for all sorts of things: trash can liners, dog poop bags, general storage, etc. So if they do not get these for free while shopping they have to buy bags and when you buy bags you buy for quality — thus not only are you buying the equivalent number of bags — you are buying thicker bags. Thus more plastic and more plastic bags.

2. Stores that cannot offer plastic bags still have to offer consumers alternative options: paper bags (the product of forests being turned into tree farms plus lots of chemicals), or cloth reusable bags. These cloth bags are made from cotton — our biggest crop and also our most toxic crop. And reusable heavy duty plastic bags — well, even more plastic. So now we have added at least three increased streams of problematic manufacturing.

3. Not only haven't you cut down on pollution, you have used up huge amounts of the community's collective energy to get make change happen, but you have only made things worse. Which in itself leads to a cycle of resignation and or the renewed hunt for the "real" culprit.

But there is no "real" culprit — *it is a systems problem.* Systems are surprising and almost always work counter to our intuition. To innovate, to invent, and to be creative — which is to say to make some kind of difference in the world, no matter the scale, we need to take into account how systems (and not discreet things) behave.

creativity happens across assemblages

Things do not appear alone — they are always part of a system — connected to other things, practices, habits, environments and purposes — which is to say that ultimately things cohere, emerge from, and circle back into a coherent ecosystem *or world.* When we work on anything we both work as and on an assemblage: we are using tools, practices, concepts, specific environments, habits, modes of organizing, etc. It is critical to recognize that to innovate at the level of a change in kind you have to develop a novel "task-space" — a specific system, environment and assemblage that will let you have an impact.

Probing, testing, following hunches, purturbating systems and following exaptive affordances is not a one-off activity, it needs to be connected to an ecosystem organized towards its "success." This is the development of the right environment, assemblage, and task-space.

It is important to remember that in all assemblages there are clear and explicit parts and a vast sea of tacit and implicit parts, practices, and activities — don't ignore the tacit.

creativity is worldmaking

To radically innovate at a systems level— to make a change in kind emerge is to co-evolve with a novel world. With any radical change-in-kind there co-emerges an ontologically new world.

Critical to all disruptive change is the practice and process of worldmaking.

Here we can return to our initial framing of change as a double loop of change-in-degree giving rise to change-in-kind and vice versa. In addition to understanding the differences between developmental and disruptive change, we have to consider the unique aspects *within* each.

Disruptive forms of change are categorically different from developmental change. While we experience and participate in developmental changes continuously, we have far less experience with disruptive change. And it is quite common to consider disruptive change simply a bigger, stronger and more radical version of developmental change. So often disruptive change is imaged as an extreme form of creativity where one simply breaks all the rules or just does crazy things — but disruptive change has a clear logic and process that can be understood and followed.

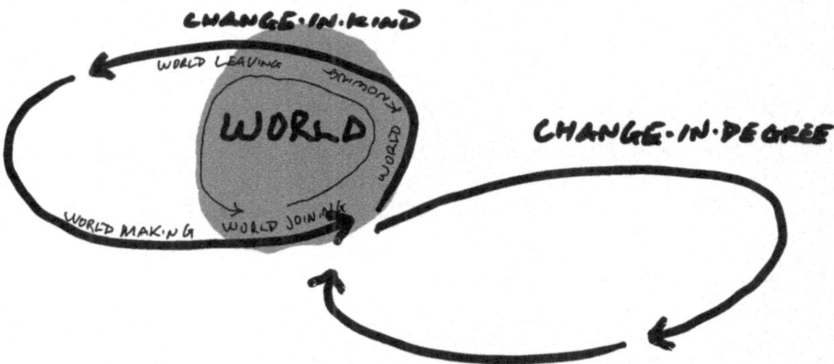

To properly understand disruptive change we have to understand that it is a qualitative change. A qualitative change can be best understood as a *change in worlds.* The shift from horse transportation to automobiles is a good example: cars did not simply replace horses as the common means of transportation. Cars and all that they entail (resource extraction, roads, motors, mass transportation, mental models, new industries, huge corporations, new nation-states, habits, etc.), gave us a new world far different from the world of relying on and living with other creatures. These two worlds (horse world vs car world) while having some outward similarities are categorically (qualitatively) different. With this insight into changes in worlds we can properly define disruptive innovation as an act of worldmaking. There are many examples of worldmaking innovations: writing, the wheel, domesticating plants and animals, God and Gods, evolutionary theory, capitalism, electricity, the internal combustion engine, contraceptives, the evolution of life, Polynesian navigation techniques — the list is long...

What counts as a disruptive change? The answer is both simple and ambiguous: anything could end up becoming a qualitative change — but we would only know in retrospect, based upon its level of qualitative change. (Disruptive innovations produce novel worlds which, by definition, cannot be known in advance).

All disruptive innovations are a rolling of the dice — we cannot know what they will become, do or mean in advance — all we can do is participate in their making. (This is an emergent process that Evan Thompson refers to as "laying down the path in walking.")

At the heart of the Innovation Design Approach is this process of qualitative change and worldmaking — which we can now add to our basic double-loop diagram:

Now that we have a sense of the two forms of change and the role of worldmaking, we can ask the question: *how does one get to the point of making a new world?* The first part of the answer is that you have to disclose and understand the underlying logic of the world that you are currently in — for without a critical understanding of the current world it is most likely that our creative actions will simply continue to reproduce this world.

Hence, prior to actually innovating, a critical practice is Disclosure. Disclosure is no easy task as the worlds that we inhabit are almost totally invisible to us — we simply take them to be "reality". And if anything outside or different from our world should appear to us it appears most often as something illogical, absurd, plain wrong, even totally impossible, or simply invisible. Difficulties aside, we can now see that there are at least three distinct phases to innovation:

1. Disclose (understand the world you are in)
2. Deviate (to make a novel world possible), and..
3. Emerge (make that world real).

Then, based upon our first four points about the need for deep engagement, we can add an initial phase: Engage. From this we have developed a basic process diagram that we will use throughout the book:

The Innovation Design Approach is about making a new world possible. Creativity and innovation are always about something bigger than finding and solving an existing problem. Creativity is worldmaking and in doing so old problems are less solved than rendered moot.

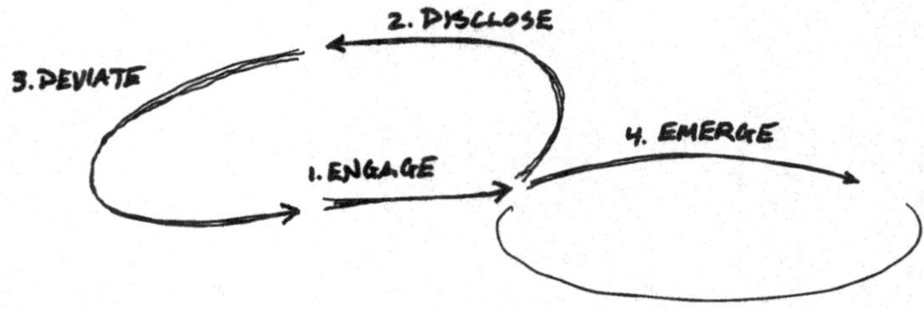

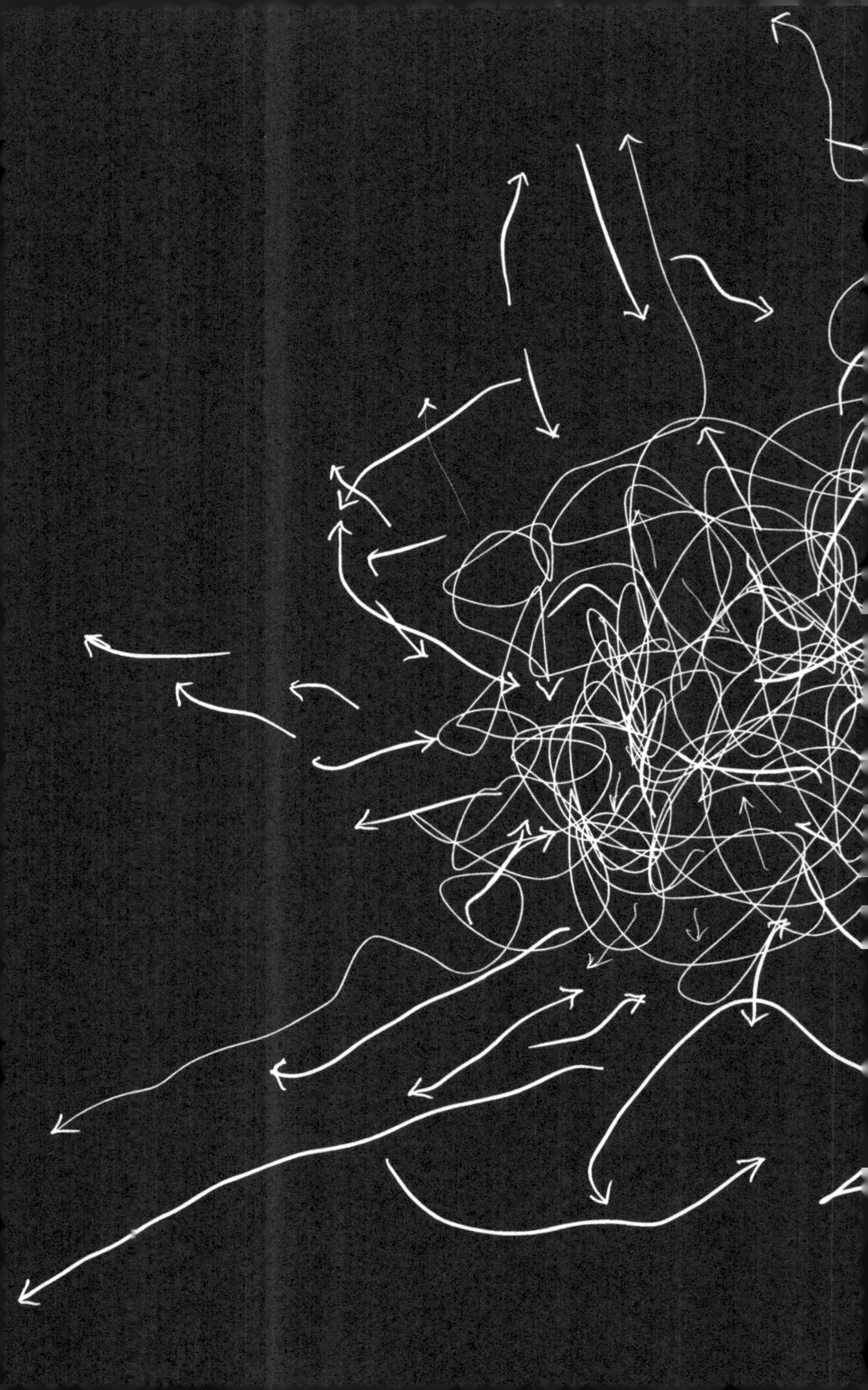

in the beginning was the event

PART FOUR: FINAL CONCEPTS (SUMMING IT UP & GETTING GOING)

SEVEN CONCEPTS TO REMEMBER AS ONE BEGINS:

1. creativity is a learned skill

So often one hears: "we are all born creative", "creativity cannot be taught, some people are just born more creative", "school beats the creativity out of us". While this sounds great, and we can all relate to these claims — after all who does not feel creative, or that some others seem far more creative? And most certainly most of us have very mixed feelings about school. But is this really the case?

I think that we should be able to see at this point in our discussion of creativity why this argument is wrong. This argument rests on a series of false assumptions:

1. Creativity is a uniquely human phenomenon
2. Creativity is a purely mental (brain-based) phenomenon
3. Brains come wired a certain way and the wiring can be improved to some degree, but ultimately you are a certain way because of your neurology, and...
4. Nature vs Nurture (born that way vs learned to be that way)

Are all valid ways to frame the human nature and learning debate. While it should be obvious, based upon the previous sections that these assumptions are wrong, what matters more is that *they are beside the point:* creativity is a worldly practice and as such — like all other worldly practices, we can learn to join it and further: learn practices that support its likelihood of happening and continuing. And it follows that creativity is learned.

This should be great news: practices to foster novel outcomes can be learned. To be creative is to participate constructively in worldly creativity. This requires many skills from the conceptual to the physical. More important than debating endlessly

Nature vs Nurture it is best to get on with the important contemporary task of innovating. This is what the Innovation Design Approach strives to develop: To think differently, we first have to act and live differently — and this will always be a collective and more-than-human project.

The Innovation Design Approach also recognizes that the above model of embodied doing leading to embodied knowing is, by itself, *not sufficient for developing creative outcomes*. Doing something different requires concrete practices that block and experiment beyond the explicit and implicit logic of the given. And doing this requires learning, and just as importantly *unlearning*, many habits, practices, concepts, histories, etc.

2. Creativity is negative to become a positive

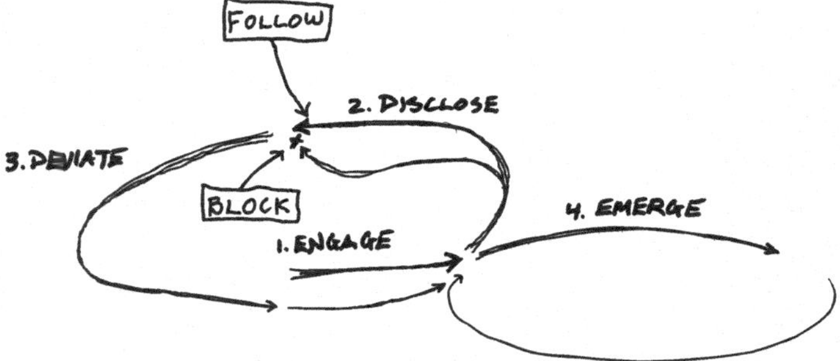

The historical image of creativity and invention is a state of being free — free of all the limits, constraints, rules put on us. Freedom and creativity are seen as synonymous — creativity is the state in which you are finally liberated from everything that holds you back and able to do precisely what one wants.

This model of creativity is based on a false opposition between order and freedom. But we know from our previous sections that creativity involves the double act of (1) knowing what is going on (disclosing), and (2) then *not* doing this (deviating).

This second phase can be confused with a "just be free" approach. But it is all about rules — negative rules: you need to *stop doing* what has been done before — and this means developing rules to *block* you from repeating the past. These rules are constraints that are generative. If we put in place a rule to block using brushes to paint we open up the field of painting to radical new possibilities. And the better, more carefully, and more thorough we develop these blockages, the more radical and novel the outcome will be. A creative process is only as good as what it refuses.

Creativity and innovation do not involve getting rid of all constraints once and for all, rather they need constraints. Rules are paradoxically liberating. The beginning of the move from disclosing to deviating is blocking. The process of blocking involves inventing and collaborating with new generative constraints in such a way as to lead to novel outcomes. Rules matter, the issue is how to make them.

3. creativity is problem producing

Rather than defining creativity as a "freedom from" (the freedom from all limits) or the outcome of a perfect idea (the liberty + brilliance model of creativity) we define creativity "problematically" and focus on the generative process of transformation, which is driven by constraints and the questions or problems they generate. The creative process is driven by problems and the fields of possibilities they generate.

Creativity is the outcome of a set of practices that lead us to invent and pose new and profound world making problems. To make sense of this we need to take a brief detour into the world of problems and questions.

What is a problem? In a very simple sense, we could say that it is the stating of a question. The structure of a question or problem contains within it the possibility of an answer or solution. The question necessarily precedes the answer — if you cannot articulate the question then no answer can be generated. Solutions are always connected to the question that generated them. Thus being able to create a problem is a generative act, and one that already encompasses the possibility of the answers that might eventually emerge.

Henri Bergson frames the role of problems in creativity this way, "It is a question of finding the problem... even more than of solving it. For a speculative problem is solved as soon as it is properly stated".

This is quite a radical statement — think of our K-12 education system with its focus on giving students questions to solve and solely focusing on the quality of the answers. Bergson flips this model on its head: what matters is the generation of a question because in the question "a solution already exists then, although it may remain hidden and, so to speak, covered up: the only thing left to do is uncover it".

Problems already contain, in a hidden manner, their solution. How can this be? The first part of the answer is quite general: If we pose a problem, say "how can we support the human body in repose?" we will have generated an immanent space in which every mode of sitting, lying, leaning will eventually emerge and find a place. But this is far too vague to be of much use — we could be waiting a very long time for anything to come of such a general question. Bergson offers us an important clue "a speculative problem is solved as soon as it is properly stated."

What is a properly stated question? Questions/problems come to us embedded in a network of unspoken assumptions, approaches and practices that frame and support the way the question/problem is posed. As we bring these into the light we see the actual contours of the problem. The more we dig into these assumptions (the "world" that we discussed above), the more we can see how critical it is to both uncover our assumptions and frame the problem/question in the best manner possible. Thus a properly stated question would articulate what is hidden — and block the assumptions that limit the new from emerging.

Solutions to problems are what we would call inventions. An example: a chair is one solution or invention to the problem (question), "How can we support the human body in repose?" The chair is a (now) very standard solution to the question. A chair accepts a problem as it is currently framed by our conventions and habits. This mode of taking a problem as given (with all of its hidden assumptions in place) leads to a "change-in-degree" solution (e.g. perhaps our chair is a "better" chair with some unique feature). But, Bergson is not simply interested in elucidating the structure of existing problems — quite the opposite, for Bergson the most important aspect of problems is that they are not fixed. Problems must be made, " stating the problem is not simply uncovering, it is *inventing*.

Discovery, or uncovering has to do with what already exists; it was, therefore, certain to happen sooner or later. Invention gives being to what did not exist; it might never have happened... The effort of invention consists of most often by raising the problem, in creating the terms it is stated". In inventing and radically reframing a problem we move from the world of "it will happen sooner or later" to one of true novelty (change-in-kind). Perhaps the biggest mistake in innovation is that far too often we assume problems as they are stated. All radical innovation involves inventing the problem — either through a radical reframing, or through the development of a totally new question.

Creativity is problematic. We are inventing new problems to develop new worlds that can lead to novel outcomes. If it were only that easy! This is not the end of the story, "the truly great problems are set forth only when they are solved." We cannot ignore the previous key arguments about creativity, and simply replace brainstorming answers with questions! When we are trying to be radically inventive, we can know what we do not want, but since the new does not yet exist *it resists all formalization* — even into a problem statement. Thus when pursuing a disruptive path of innovation we might know what not to do (or what to block), but we need to experimentally allow the problem to co-emerge with our experiments. The goal then of blocking and experimenting is not to produce a solution or even an alternative world — that only comes much, much later — first we need to generate a portal, an opening, an experimental path — and this is where the blocking of old assumptions and the generating of novel quasi-questions will help us in deviating. Later we will come to understand what our actual novel question is...

4. creativity is not neutral

Creativity has a history. Why in this moment of increasingly precarious forms of work, and the ever-widening disparity between the ultra-wealthy and everyone else are we all being encouraged to be more flexible, creative and innovative?

In whose service are these ideas and values?

Creativity and innovation are inherently loaded issues. We need to think critically about our contemporary reality. Are we being creative just to make new trendy widgets? Or are new worlds possible? What are we trying to sustain? What is really needed?

The Innovation Design Approach sees that the creativity, invention, and innovation that we champion are not neutral goods. We live in a very dangerous moment which requires both caution and innocence. Everything, as Foucault said, is dangerous, and new worlds are possible. But, this does not mean we champion creativity and the new above all else, we need a critical visionary creativity that understands that we are not separate from all the consequences of what emerges from what we initiate.

5. creativity never begins from zero

Get out of your head, get out of your studio, get out of your ideas, get out of your brainstorming session and join the world — engage, probe, experiment.

You do not need a clean slate — and this will never be possible — embrace the complexity of things, work with others, surrender to the process: co-emerge and co-evolve from this world here and now.

We promise — interesting, surprising and worthwhile

things will happen — they just won't be what any of us expected — but, hey — that is a really really good thing!

6. creativity has no method

As you read this it would be very easy to mistake the Innovation Design Approach for a capital M "Method." Innovation Design is not a Method, but a set of pragmatic tools and procedures. Why bring this up? There is an easy dogmatism and false sense of security in Methods, which in their one-size-fits-all exuberance can all-too-readily squash curiosity, difference, possibilities and ultimately innovation. Whitehead, says it well, "Some of the major disasters of mankind have been produced by the narrowness of men with a good methodology."

Today, Methods of innovation abound. Design Thinking and the Lean Canvas are just two of the most popular Methods being taught on a global scale such that their limits and problems as Methods have become obvious. Despite this, or perhaps because of it, they remain an entrenched dogmatic force in the world of innovation.

The Innovation Design Approach, as a set of skills, should not be mistaken for a one-size-fits-all Method. We are trying the best we can to avoid the limits and blind spots of Methods -- whether historical models or more recent user-centered models such as Design Thinking, by offering an open and flexible set of practices combined with a philosophical outlook. What looks like a Method in this document is an attempt to do two distinct, and possibly contradictory things, (1) develop new creative processes/tools for innovation and (2) find a way to teach these in a simple manner. (If you wish to insist upon calling it a method then it is only in the sense that Herman Melville claims for himself, "There are some enterprises in which a careful disorderliness is the true method.")

Our aversion to Methods should not be mistaken for a willingness to offer a laissez-faire approach. Innovation Design has a distinct style of creativity Innovation Design puts experimental worldmaking at the core of innovation in contrast to most western models of innovation and design that have focused on generating ideas, and solutions.

We believe that innovation, at its most creative, is a worldmaking and not an idea or product making practice. Innovations are assemblages of novel deeply embodied practices, tools, implicit mentalities, concepts, environments and goals. It is this assemblage that what we are calling a "world." Experimental worldmaking is a fundamentally engaged, responsive and emergent practice that re-orients creativity towards an embedded, co-evolving, problem producing, worldmaking and systems based practice. In short it is a hands-on worldly and experimental action-oriented collaborative approach.

If creativity is not pre-existing in the head then it depends wholly on practice — why some people are more "creative" is simply because they have practiced and fully embodied techniques of the innovation process. This goes for organizations, collectives and events — practice matters.

This philosophical critique and alternative focus is not about winning an intellectual debate about the definition of creativity, it matters deeply because our most pressing issues today from climate change to equality are complex, dynamic, systemic and open-ended problems that cannot be effectively addressed (and have often been caused or exacerbated) by narrow, linear solution centric methods of design and innovation.

Let's invent problems worth having for worlds worth making!

7. creativity requires us to fundamentally rethink who we are

Enough said — this should be obvious by now — and hopefully you are already changed and rethinking some fundamental things...

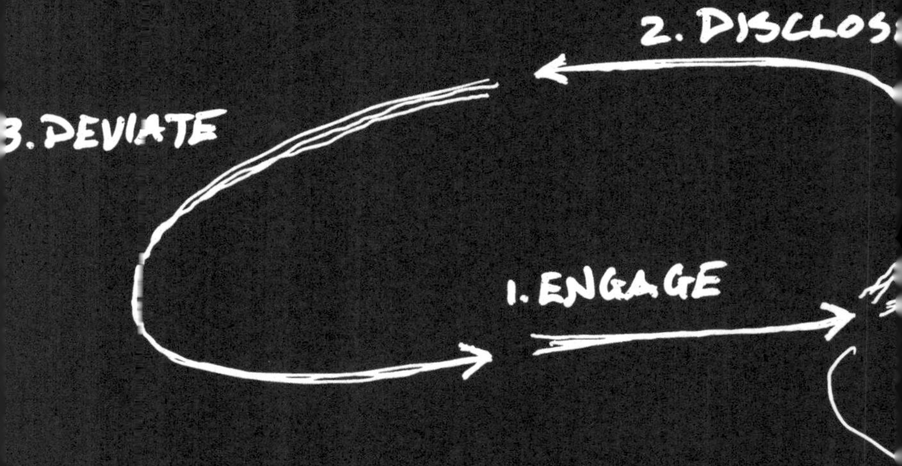

2. DISCLOS

3. DEVIATE

1. ENGAGE

engage

disclose

deviate

4. EMERGE

emerge

HOW TO INNOVATE: THE TASKS AND PRACTICES

THE FOUR TASKS OF INNOVATION DESIGN

Over the years, as we researched and developed our understanding of innovation, it has always been directly tied to the practical activity of actually innovating.

Working on projects from wetland remediation to developing new learning models have been our testing grounds. With each project came a new experiment in evolving a better innovation process.

While we realized early on that the classical three step process of ideate, plan and make (and all of its countless variations) would never lead to innovation, it took us much longer to develop a powerful alternative holistic process.

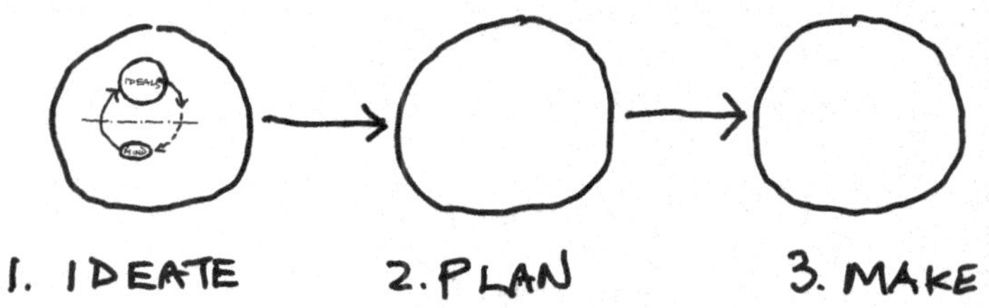

Working on many highly diverse projects has forced us to develop many discreet tools and practices that answered specific innovation roadblocks.

How to:

- do real experiments for novelty
- disclose and block the known
- engage and follow the unintended
- develop alternative worlds
- be far more embodied and rely on know-how over know-what

These tools were enormously helpful. But innovation is not simply about deploying a set of powerful tools in an ad hoc method — it is about the sequencing of a coherent process.

As our understanding evolved, so too did our process. We have been articulating, testing, and remaking this process through countless iterations. Even when we thought we had it all perfectly worked out — to the point we designed and had a series of posters printed — the surprising nature of innovation itself forced us back to the lab to continue honing the process. (We still have the stack of posters to remind us of our own hubris).

For the last five years we've continued refining our process of innovation that consists of four tasks:

1. Engage
2. Disclose
3. Deviate
4. Emerge

These four tasks can be thought of as a set of interconnected practices or activities. Each takes on a distinct aspect of the innovation process:

- **Engage** and **Disclose** are the tasks necessary to prepare for innovation,
- **Deviate** and **Emerge** are the two distinct processes that foster the two distinct forms of change:
    - change-in-degree (Emerge), and
    - change-in-kind (Deviate).
- While **Deviate** fosters a disruptive change, which comes early in the process,
- **Emerge** as a developmental process, always comes at the end to make things real.

Hence the sequential order of (1) Engage, (2) Disclose, (3) Deviate, (4) Emerge.

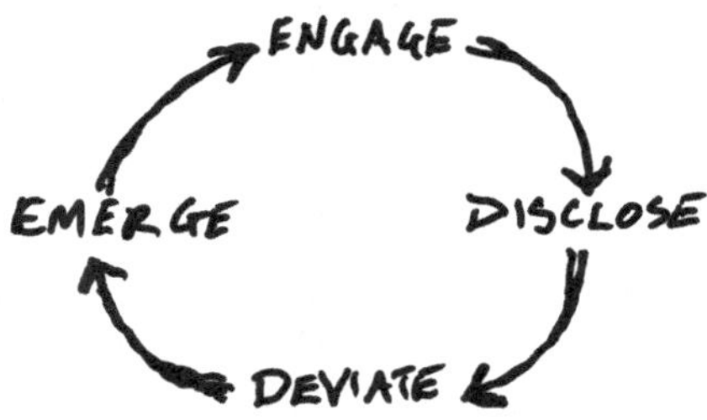

Even though these are interconnected tasks where one flows to the next, diagramming this, or any innovation process, as circular is, as we realized when we had those posters printed, a huge mistake.

With a circle we immediately lose sight of the fact that there are two radically distinct processes at the heart of innovation:

1. change-in-degree (developmental change), and
2. change-in-kind (disruptive change)

... each of which requires a wholly distinct process. And each moving in a wholly different direction.

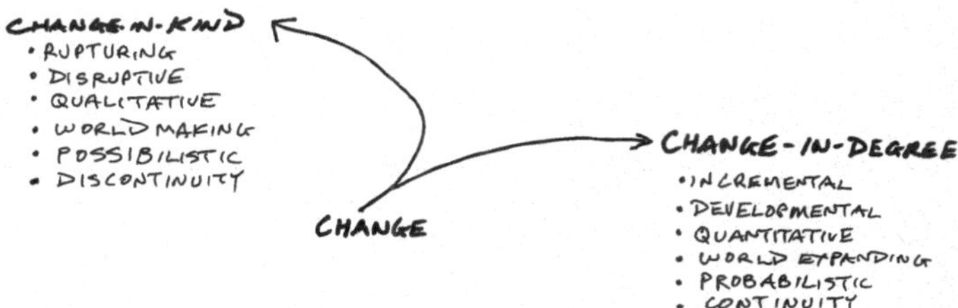

Remembering this, made us realize that innovation is not circular — it is composed of two connected loops going in opposite directions.

The loop of Deviation points *backward* and the loop of Emerge points *forward*.

Developing or improving something degree by degree is a progressive and forward moving process. And disruption and the development of a whole new approach is to rupture this forward movement of progress. This needs to be shown and understood as two distinct but connected loops:

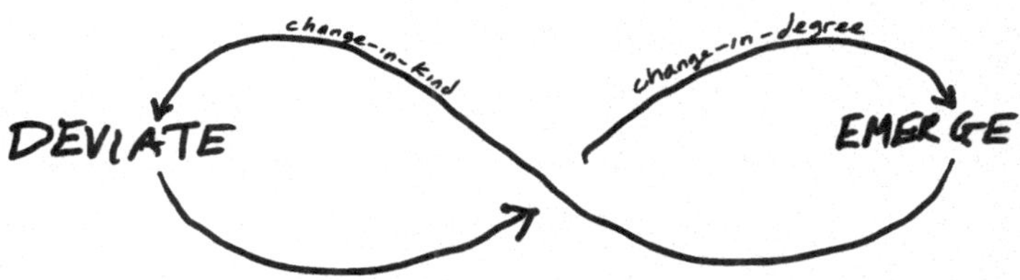

Understanding the two distinct pathways of innovation still leaves the key question unanswered: *How to begin?*

All activity of change begins by leaving your office, leaving your studio — getting out of your head and joining with the world in a fully engaged manner.

In this way we don't start by ideating, empathizing or innovating, we start by immersing ourselves deeply in an ongoing reality. Therefore, the **Engage** phase begins the process.

From engagement we find ourselves at a true crossroads — we have to decide:

- are we interested in developing within the context of what already exists?
- or do we wish to be more radical and develop something that is truly novel?

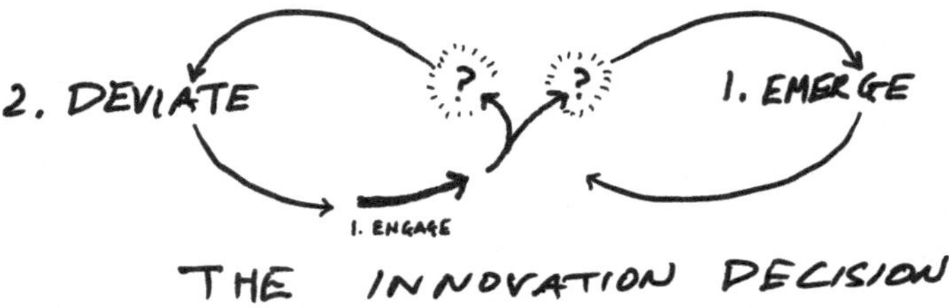

Thus we show engage as moving both:

- *forward* to continue into a developmental innovation process (**Emerge**):
- *stepping backwards* from the forward rush of progress to pause and understand the deep hidden logic of your current reality (**Disclose**) and enter into a process of **Deviation** from that reality:

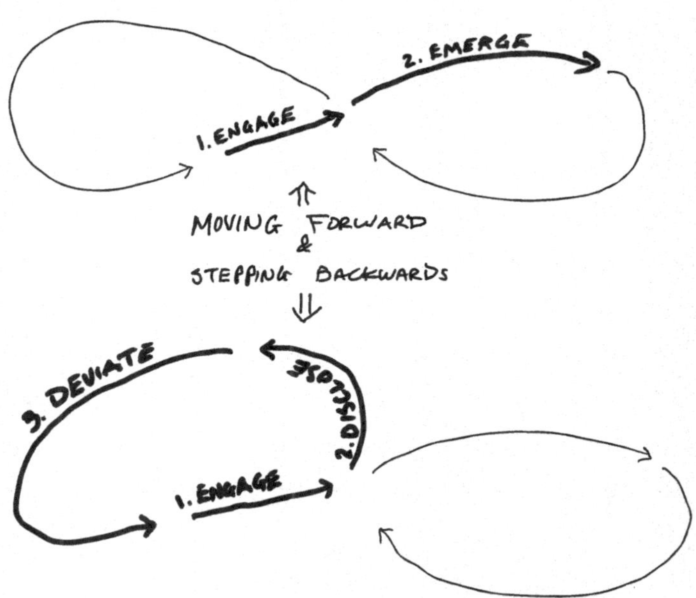

While **Engagement, Deviation** and **Emergence** are simplest to understand and often get all the attention — it is **Disclosure** that is key to everything in innovation. No matter what you do — you will never develop a deep and disruptive paradigm busting worldmaking innovation if you do not uncover and block a series of existing practices, habits and worlds.

With a basic understanding of these four phases and how they connect to the two loops of change we can lay out a simple diagram of the full process:

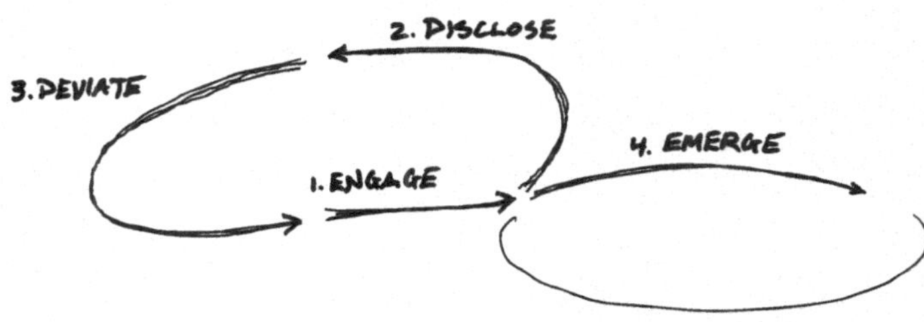

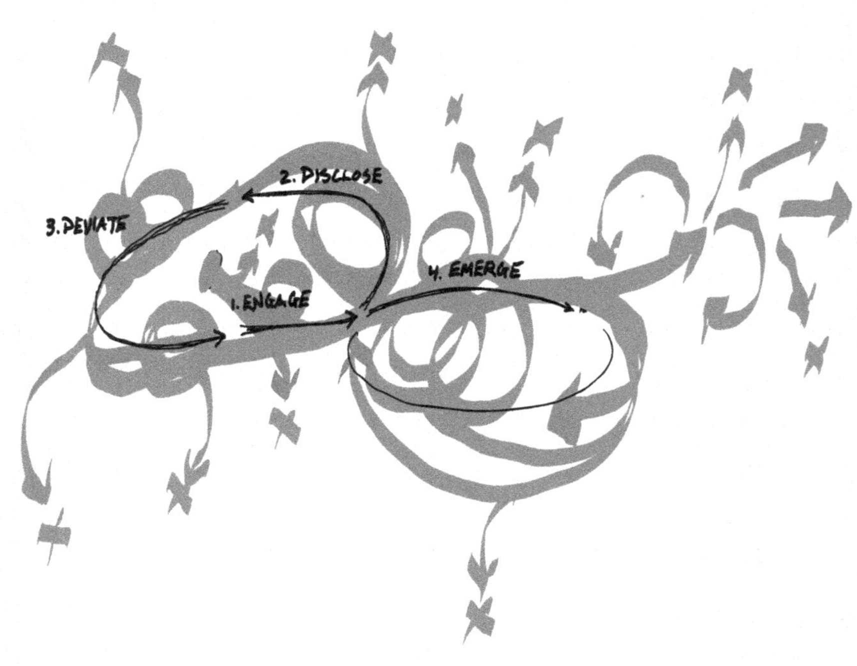
2. DISCLOSE
3. DEVIATE
4. EMERGE
1. ENGAGE

GETTING MORE DETAILED: THE 15 PRACTICES OF INNOVATION

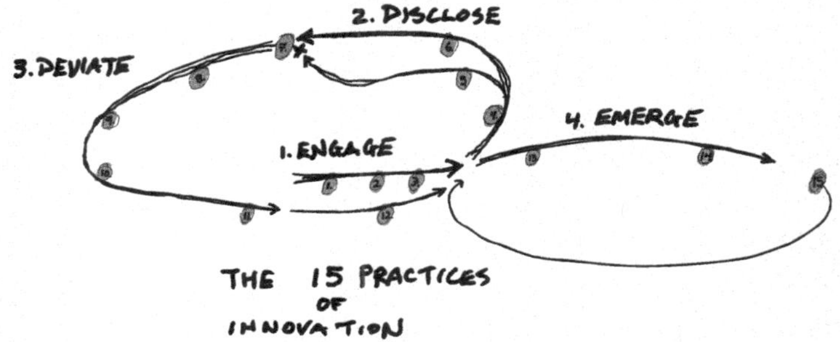

Once oriented to the big picture we can now move into the detailed process of innovation. While we can think of the innovation process as one where we move through four general tasks, what we are really doing is a series of sequential practices. Innovation is ultimately a journey — a strange and surprising journey of twists and turns, many dead-ends, strange leaps, shocks, moments of great beauty and wonderment, a lot of mundane work, and what might seem like endless repetition — all with the goal of making something emerge that is wholly unexpected (see diagram on left-hand page...).

There are fifteen distinct practices, roughly 3-5 in each task. Each practice consists of a number of distinct research programs, experiments and questions. In the next section of the book we will lay out in detail how to engage with each task and their related practices, but for now an overview will help introduce the actual work of innovation.

ENGAGE

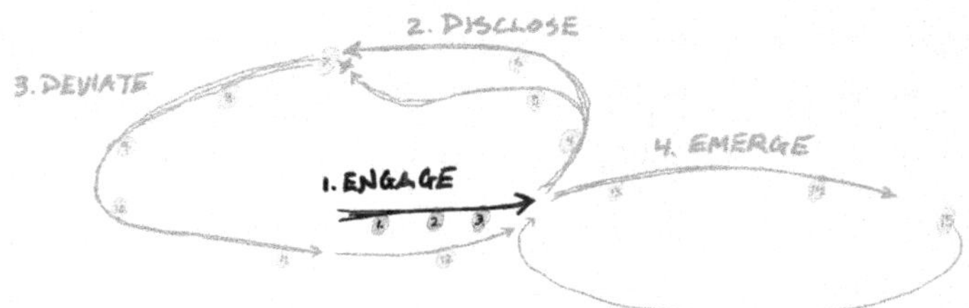

The Engage task is both the initial steps in the process of innovation and the beginning of a practice of deep engagement that continues throughout all of the phases of innovation.

In a certain sense the engage phase is about learning how to leave the secure and known and join the flow of life. It is about getting out of your head and getting out of your comfort zone and engaging. Not much in life, never mind innovation, will happen without doing this.

Often there is a strong temptation to skip this step, we assume we already know all the answers and can move on to the real work of innovating. But the full immersion into a world and a question with others builds a shared ecosystem — a commons that becomes the expansive well that novelty can, in all its surprising glory, emerge.

We divide this task up into three practices, which while presented as being sequential, are ultimately deeply interwoven:

1. Opening & Grounding: Why and where one begins an innovation journey is truly diverse. Sometimes it is an idea, at other times a vexing question, or perhaps an observation, or a persistent problem. You can begin anywhere. When you begin matters little, it is how you go that counts. This task begins that process by both opening you up to the larger space of the question and grounding you in the lived world of that question.

2. Attuning & Gathering: As you ground yourself in a question it is important to connect with others — to participate and engage in the world surrounding your area of interest. Develop a collaborative community. What do they do? What is their history? What are their concerns? How can you make a shared space of curiosity?

3. Pattern Recognition: As one dwells in the larger world of a question and connects with a community equally entangled in this question the collective activity of uncovering the underlying logics, habits, histories and trends can begin.

DISCLOSE

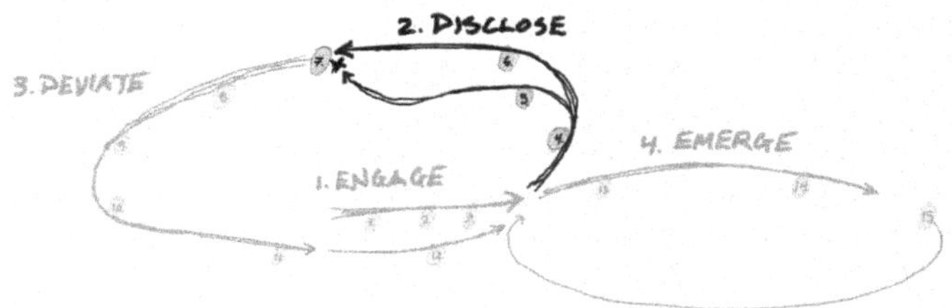

Disclosure is a continuation of the Pattern Recognition activity that ended the Engage task. But in this new task of Disclosure the critical activity of uncovering is only half of what we seek to discover.

What is unique about the Disclosure is that it splits into two distinct parallel paths. One path focuses on a critical uncovering of the implicit logic of current practices, and the other path focuses on discovering and exploring unintentional possibilities. It is these two wholly distinct parallel activities that will allow for disruptive innovation to emerge in the next task: Deviation.

4. Defining: By critically interrogating the scope, history, and implicit logic of one's question during the task of Engage, one is now prepared to define the larger "matter of concern" in regards to which your question is simply one historically contingent approach. Grasping that you're concerned with something bigger than a question or framework allows you to release yourself from your narrow focus on the question, problems and solutions— and ultimately open yourself up to the possibility that there is a whole other way of being alive that might not even contain this question, issue or problem. This activity could be equally well named as "releasement".

5. Uncovering: Innovation cannot begin to get novel if it stops at uncovering a history or discovering trends, it needs to go deeper. What is the framework, paradigm or even world that gives rise to a way of being alive that evolves these issues, questions, problems and practices? It is only when this question is answered at an *ontological level* that one can begin to innovate in a profound manner.

We do this because we know that other worlds are possible and the goal of innovation is the realization of another world.

6. Exploration (towards the unintended): Parallel to uncovering the underlying logics of your issue/question you need to discover unintended possibilities within the objects, environments, habits and frameworks entangled with your broad area of interest (which you discovered and joined in during the Emerge task). These unintended possibilities are what will drive your disruptive innovation experiments in the next task of innovation: Deviate.

DEVIATE

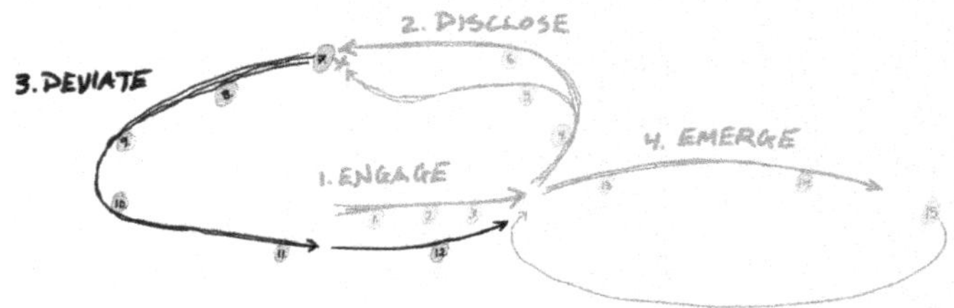

The task of Deviation is to deliberately put the known path aside and co-emerge a novel and new path via considered experimentation.

The goal of Deviation is not to come up with a solution or a product — that comes much later in the process. The goal of Deviation is to develop a new and novel approach to your matter of concern.

This "approach" can range in scope from a radical but small scale innovation to something paradigm busting and truly worldmaking.

Here, during the task of Deviation, the ontological new emerges via a process of exaptive design. While the multiple practices of Engage and Disclose are holistic and do overlap, with Deviate that is not the case, it is important to do these sequentially.

7. Staging: *This involves two things: (1)*

1. defining the scope and scale of what can change, and
2. deciding what to block and what to follow.

It is here that one sets up what Erin Manning calls the "enabling constraint" — that which you refuse. This comes out of the activity of Uncovering.

Ideally one blocks or refuses a paradigm or world. Such a blocking will potentially lead to the greatest possible novelty.

As critical as what is blocked is the question of what is followed. This grows out of the activity of Exploration where promising unintended possibilities have been discovered. Once the initial conditions blocking and following are staged it is time to move onto the activity of Experimentation.

8. Experimenting: With what is blocked and what will be followed in place one carries out a series of experiments, following, stabilizing and co-emerging unintended possibilities.

These experiments follow what we term the Exaptive Innovation Process. This involves a series of iterative experiments in blocking and following that move one ever further into the unknown — the new and novel.

9. Transversal Articulation: As the practice of experimentation progresses one needs to take stock from the perspective of the emergent novelty that is being developed.

As humans we are deeply connected to our past and the reasons for what we do and did. This practice allows us to step out of that history and past and see the new for what it is and what it could be. We are pausing to articulate our transversal (sideways) moves in their full radicality so we can continue to experiment, but from the perspective of what is being born.

10. Worlding: The preceding practices lead one into an emerging novel paradigm/world. Worlds are not discovered but co-emerged and co-evolved.

Now it is time to pause the experiments and attempt to collectively articulate what new approach and what new world is beginning to emerge. This practice is both speculative and ontological. The crux is to keep the emergent difference alive and not reduce the possible to the merely probable. The articulation of worlding is also the articulation of tools, practices, embodiments and territories (it is not an idea). A novel assemblage is forming.

Worlding: one can think of the entire process of innovation as this task.

The danger is to see this activity as "ideation" where a vision of the future is made and that everything from this point forward is just planning and executing on this vision. That would be to fall back into the "God model" of innovation.

The activity of worlding does not magically produce a world but builds out an emergent path into a possible territory that will later take on a life of its own.

[Ouroboros: Quite often the activity of worlding falls back into the known. This is to be expected. Radical innovation is difficult. The activity of Ouroboros is to assist in pushing your emergent novelty further via a series of paradoxical techniques where the world turns upon itself and emerges as another.]

11. Strategic Joining: Other worlds are possible and yes other worlds can be speculatively developed. But, how does this have a meaningful transformative impact on our reality? Strategic Joining seeks to begin to test answers and possible pathways to transformational impact.

EMERGE

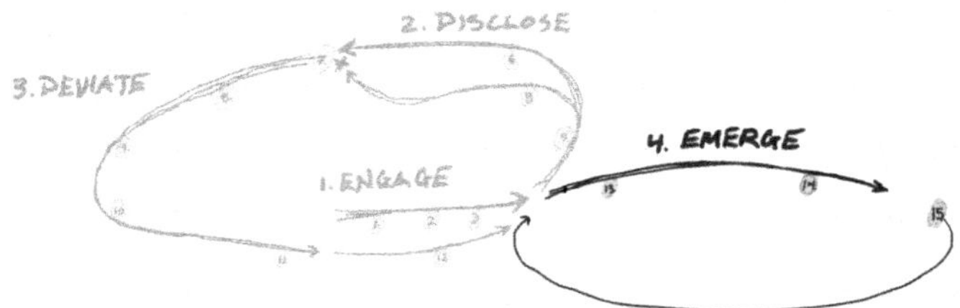

The task of emergence is to make the radical possibilities drawn forth into a nascent state of existence during Deviation real, concrete and impactful. This is a highly strategic and experimental phase where the goal is no longer to deviate but to make the deviations transform our current reality.

This happens by probing and testing and co-evolving both a community and a "product". This "product" — whatever it might be — a thing, a service, an event — is ultimately an ecosystem. And it is the ecosystem's emergence and ever evolving state of thriving that is the "goal" of Emerge. The practices of Emerge are sequential and highly iterative — to make anything emerge and become transformative is to test, shift and repeat; many, many times.

12. Emergent Transition: Emergence begins by transitioning from a world of qualitative change to the world of developmental change. Slowly a concrete ecosystem needs to be developed.

During the activity of transition one probes and tests critical points in existing systems to see how it responds. These unique and unpredictable responses guide the process as they reveal emergent pathways and leverage points in the system. In the activity of probing a new collective — a new community and culture begins to configure around the activity.

13. Coevolution: Things are starting to cohere in surprising ways: new practices are emerging alongside a budding community and culture. It is this nascent ecosystem that one needs to co-evolve into an ever more stable and fully realized state.

There is a relay that emerges between people, practices,

tools, ideas, and values that is leading towards the founding of new ways of doing and being. Much of this will be a surprise. The practices of coevolution need to embrace these surprises and transform along with them.

14. Ecosystem Building: Novel worlds are not ideas — they are coherent and stable assemblages of interconnected networks of tools, practices, resources, values, and communities.

Great care and attention has to be given to supporting and stabilizing this as it emerges in a "spontaneous" manner. Ecosystem building is this practice and in a very real sense the practices of Coevolution and Ecosystem Building never end — things persist because we make it possible.

15. Amplification: The effectiveness of any system relies on many amplifying and reinforcing feedback loops. These need to loop into new territories and possibilities as well as loop-back deeper into the process. Ideally one is looping back into the Disruptive task to renew the novel potentials of your ecosystem.

[Feedback: When nearing the end of a task it is critical to set up a more formal check-in or feedback session. This should be designed in a manner that is specific to the context.*]*

HOW TO HACK THE INNOVATION DESIGN PROCESS

While we just wrote out the process of innovation as an almost linear singular step by step process — there is no one proper way through the loops of innovation.

Innovation has no fixed starting point. Innovation has no fixed path. And ultimately innovation has no proper endpoint.

Where you start and how you proceed is entirely dependent on where you are and where you are trying to go.

Equally where you start and where you end up can be determined by many outside forces.

While we recommend, for the sake of learning the total process of innovation, that you follow this workbook from beginning to end, know that the linear step by step process will rarely be the innovation journey you take.

Once you understand the process you can jump to the phase that best suits your needs, and develop a novel pathway.

For the sake of demonstrating the flexibility and possibilities of the process lets look four common pathways through the innovation process:

1. You have a clear understanding of what you wish to develop:

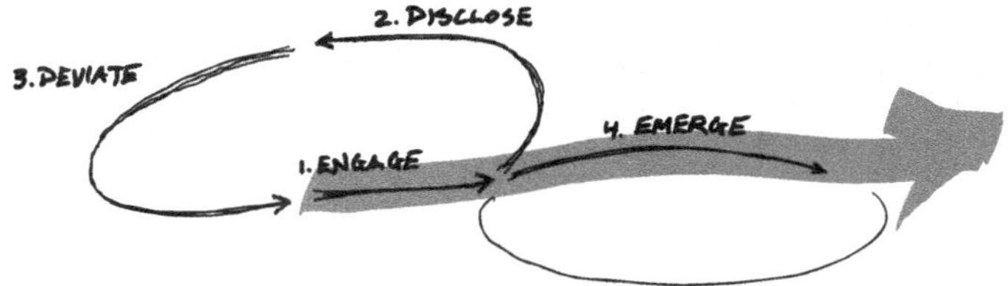

This is the path of most entrepreneurs and designers. When you have a clear idea about what you wish to make you can start with Engage and then move directly to Emerge.

While this path often seems the fastest and most straightforward — don't be fooled: the process is loopy -- you are going backwards - iterating, testing, revising, changing often.

The advantages of this path is its directness, the dangers of this path is that we end up with a one-off product — we never fully develop an ecosystem nor realize the world expanding or world grounding possibilities of what we are making. We call this being "world-blind" and it is the fate of many an inventor.

The answer to the problem of being world-blind is to loop through the disclose phase to see what world your emerging novel concept is co-evolving (inventing) along-side of.

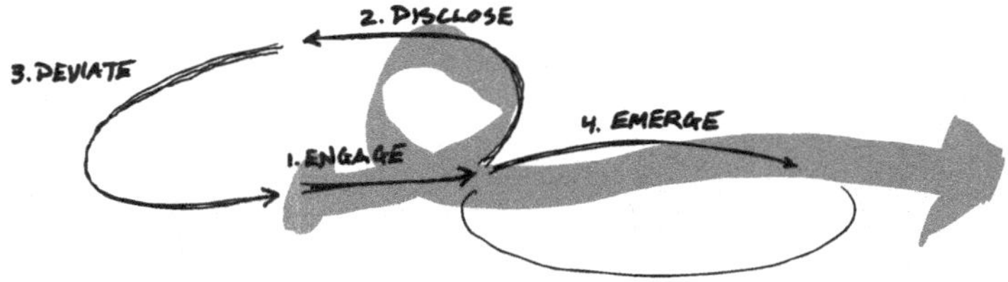

2. You have an existing product or service to evolve:

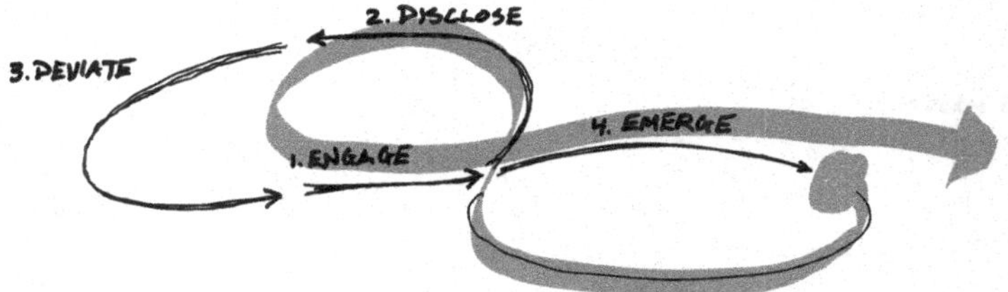

Often one already has a product or service in circulation, and the question is how does one enrich a (narrow) innovation (your solution) into a resilient (business) ecosystem or a more robust solution?

Or perhaps you are simply interested in developing what could come next out of what you have already done.

For this you are beginning at the "end" of the Emerge phase and looping back into the world disclosing practices of the Disclose phase. This allows you to experimentally uncover the deeper logics and richer paradigmatic potentials of your concept area. This process of deep paradigmatic uncovering moves one away from a narrow solution towards a resilient and robust ecosystem of multiple opportunities.

With this deep paradigmatic understanding you now move back through the Engage and Emerge tasks where you are testing out these expanded possibilities and forming a community of users. This process will then lead you into the final phase of where you develop these possibilities into a reality.

3. You wish to disrupt an existing approach:

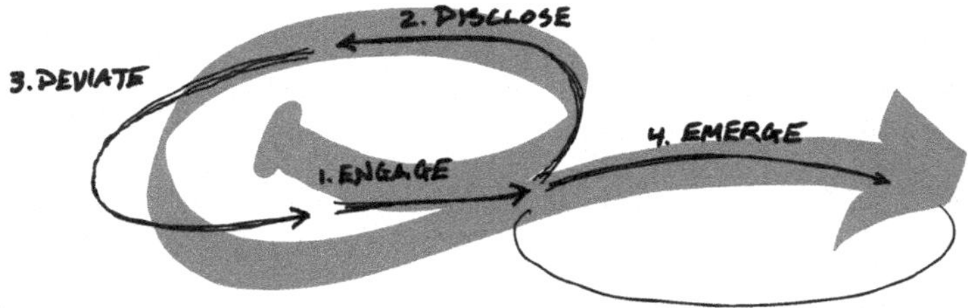

At the core of all innovation and making is the ever present potential for genuine novelty known as Disruptive Innovation.

This is where the Innovation Design Framework offers a powerful new approach: Engage, Disclose, Deviate, Emerge.

While we have already covered this in the previous section it is good to remember the process: Engagement moves backward into the uncovering of existing approaches/paradigms, and unintended possibilities which are then experimentally

Developed via a sideways process of iterative blocking and following to develop a novel world. It is only after a novel world or paradigm has been developed that one can move towards the development of problems and solutions which define classical design and entrepreneurship strategies.

4. Some Stand Alone Tools:

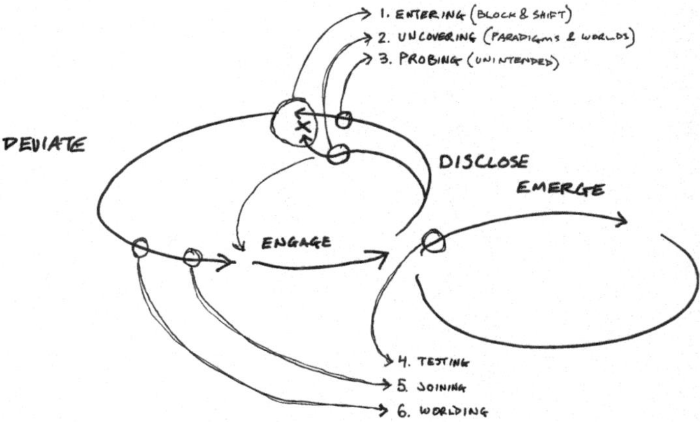

Ultimately all the various components of the innovation process can be used alone or in new non-linear connections with each other. Here are six that we use quite often and why:

1. Uncovering (Approaches, Paradigms and Worlds): Change can only really happen when one knows what is going on at a deep level. We will use these techniques in a fast manner (diagramming forms) throughout. As you get good at seeing patterns you begin to recognize ones that repeat and it becomes easier to put them aside.

2. Exploration (towards Unintended Potentials): This activity of using things in novel ways (puttering, playing and improvising) is part of our everyday lives — we are always asking: *what else can this do that was not intended?* Here too, the more one does it the more one recognizes this everywhere in life.

3. Staging and Experimenting (Block & Shift): Again an everyday technique we use constantly: block something and force yourself to act and think differently. The blockage does not need to be big, and can be fun (block utensils at dinner). Not a moment goes by when the thought of blocking something does not arise. Critical at every point of innovation.

4. Worlding: One exercise we do quite a bit is taking new and strange things and then speculating on what novel mode of being alive it suggests — what portal to novel modes of being could they open up?

Far too often we are world-blind and miss how potentially revolutionary simple things can be.

In the story of innovators it is far too often someone else that sees the worldmaking potential for something — inventors are often too close to what they make or are working under the mistaken assumption that their invention simply "solves a problem". It is important to always be aware of the alternative worldmaking potential of all things — especially the most mundane.

5. Strategic Joining (Map & Relocate &/or Re-engage): Mapping and diagramming and other forms of visual thinking are critical at every moment — reality, change and creativity are dynamic nonlinear processes that diagrams help us to visualize best. Mapping shows diverse potentials and multiple alternative pathways, this gets us out of our fixation on single answers and narrow solution paths.

6. Probing: This one step is a way of testing a system to see what might emerge. In complex highly dynamic situations probing becomes the only way to get a sense of what is going on. Probes also keep us honest and outside of "solution thinking".

REVIEW

Innovation Design brings innovation out of the mystical realms and makes it a concrete pragmatic process that can be explicated for the sake of learning in a series of steps.

This is not to claim that one can equate pragmatic with easy or a guarantee of success. One is never done learning the craft of making, and each project we undertake requires us to begin again and creatively re-invent the processes.

INNOVATION DESIGN

1. *Innovation* is production of the genuinely new

2. *Design* is a process of action towards an outcome = Innovation Design is the process for producing the genuinely new.

INNOVATION

1. The *new* is when change happens that produces a difference.
2. There are two types of difference: Difference-in-degree, and Difference-in-kind
3. These two forms of difference/change correspond to two distinct forms of Innovation: Developmental and Disruptive.
4. Developmental Innovation is incremental, world expanding, quantitative, probabilistic, and improving.
5. Disruptive is rupturing, qualitative, possibilistic, and world making.

PROCESSES FOR INNOVATION

There are four key processes that distinguishes Innovation Design:

1. **Engage:** Beginning with a matter of interest or concern actively collectively immerse yourself collectively in its world(s) in a way that evolves deep and sustained fully immersive engagement. The Engage phase requires you to foster collectivity, commons, intra-dependency, belonging and open embedded engagement. Notice patterns, trends, and trajectories as they emerge. You are staging an encounter.
2. **Disclose:** Via deep engagement (phase one) disclose the underlying logic, habits, patterns, paradigms and world of your matter of concern. Uncover multiple qualitatively different modes and pathways. In this activity notice unintended potentialities of matters and practices.
3. **Deviate:** Disruptive Innovation: begin by blocking critical aspects of an existing world, paradigm, and or habits. Then via an iterative open experimental embodied and physically grounded process of deviation evolve a radically new world or paradigm, habits and patterns. Relocate and or reconnect and develop this world in an engaged manner.
4. **Emerge:** Starting from either where you are, or beginning to develop your novel world (emerging from the previous phases), probe and iteratively co-evolve collectively to concretely realize a specific outcome.

AN ETHOS FOR APPROACHING CREATIVITY: PRACTICES FOR INNOVATION

To allow creative processes to flourish in our lives we need to change our general approach to life. Here are some suggestions:

Value:

- ...becoming over being
- ...novelty over permanence
- ...difference over identity
- ...repetition over reflection
- ...long emergence over sudden eureka moments
- ...joining, following, emerging and transforming-*with* over founding, visioning, authoring
- ...vague feeling, and sensing of what is odd and different of knowing what is clear and distinct
- ...creativity as a worldly process and not a human mental capacity
- ...experimental doing over removed ideation
- ...blocking the known and moving sideways
- ...that innovation does not set out to "solve" anything
- ...the non-linear
- ...the work of avoiding reducing things to essences, magic bullets, or origins
- ...multiplicity and variation, and integrate this into everything
- *...processes* — this means developing and following procedures
- ...collaboration and collaborations over the illusion of individuality — all great acts of innovation and creativity happened collectively — with others (and not just human others)
- ...joy, surprise, curiosity
- ...schock, disgust, horror
- ...humility and wonder

Become:

- ...alien and playful
- ...sensitive to the liberating force of life, chaos, difference and creativity over the forces of law, order, repetition, and sameness
- ...an experiment: live life as an open experimental project
- ...a transdisciplinary networker, amateur, and generalist
- ...willing to trust the process
- ...comfortable with being confused, and that we will fail, and that there will be no guarantee in what we do
- ...OK with the fact that creativity will involve radical forms of rupture and betrayal of the given
- ...a great collaborator

Understand that:

- ... you will change
- ...creation as iterative (but not linear)
- ...assemblages matter
- ...everything is "networked" and relational (without a single author, or any author)
- That the "outcome" cannot be known in advance (& is not the final "purpose")
- That the origin of anything need not have any purpose, nor does it directly relate to its current use
- That the most interesting "traits" are nonadaptive (exaptive) -they are world opening (for a world that does not yet exist)
- Making/Thinking is a conjoined practice (not thinking then making). Ideas come later.
- Treat things as being active and having agency.
- Things shape us. Tools make us. Understand how this works.
- Innovation is messy, challenges our belief in solving

problems head on, and requires a lot of seemingly "useless" experimentation

- It is going to be messy (figuratively and literally). You need dedicated spaces
- It is going to take time - which will be hard to fit into a workshop, the regular work day, or a predefined sprint. New models need to be developed
- It is not based primarily in ideas (or in the mind).
- Things play a significant active role.
- Experiments invent their own criteria, questions/problems, fields, frameworks, and worlds.
- It is emergent--it involves following: wayfinding in waymaking.
- Causality isn't linear - it is crazy
- Creativity is not a willy-nilly free-for-all — there are processes
- ...creativity is creativity leadership. We are learning and teaching how to be comfortable leading oneself and others into discomfort and open-endedness. Play. Comfort. Seeing ethos and space.

Do:

- Cross thresholds from difference-in-degree to difference-in-kind
- Utilize the non-intended capacities of things and betray their original purpose
- Co-evolve with an environment
- Make a space that protects novelty (the lab) - keeps it away from "survival of the fittest" experiments/situations - and keep it away from having to be "something" as long as possible (needs to iteratively betray multiple "identities")
- Develop pirate projects-- probes into the unknown - open ended - perturbing a field - activating emergent unknowable (in advance) potentials - and then transforming with them...
- Use things as probes and not products

- Develop ways to understand and move between differing frameworks, cosmologies & paradigms (learn, collect, develop the knowledge of alternative frameworks)
- Train oneself to limit moral or factual judgements (follow practices, and ideas with an open mind). Stop the habit of being a "devil's advocate"
- Shift your focus from thinking about what something "is" to only considering: "What can it do?" This is a key disposition to acquire to have a truly experimental approach. Once you get good at asking "what can it do?" now ask: "and what else can it do?" Don't stop at one or two options, figure out 10 or more (this is where it gets interesting)
- Treat innovation/creativity as a process not a product.
- Worldmaking before problem tackling. Problem producing not problem solving. Problem producing before solution producing.
- Engage reality as a dynamic system and not composed of discrete things.
- It is a collective process (need to work & network with others--things, ideas, cultures, creatures, humans).
- Test, experiment, observe, multiply
- Work at a systems scale
- We need to move away from thinking of creativity as a thing - especially a mysterious internal property to be "unlocked". (The genius model).
- Invent rules and follow them (it won't be pregiven)
- ...we need to overcome our sense of self. Especially that we feel inadequate. "I'm not creative." "Why bother - every form of this has already been invented, nothing new can be done." This feeling will be the beginning of any creative endeavor. Ignore it. Push on. This feeling will always be there. Remember it is not about us.

be like a crow

DOING INNOVATION

Here is our detailed step-by-step guide to doing the work of innovating. It is the formalized process of *How to Innovate.* It consists of introductions and questions and activities that take you through the four tasks of the Innovation Design Approach.

Answering these questions in a room on large sheets of poster paper is not innovation. What matters is that you do the activities — in the world, with others, evolving and changing as you go.

At the beginning a notebook will suffice to keep track of things — what you will need in terms of infrastructure, location, collaborators and practices will reveal themselves as you progress.

These questions and activities alone will not suffice — you will need to both customize and change things and you will need to look to other resources to go deep into certain areas of the process. Be pragmatic and inventive with the process.

Most of what one does in innovation is to probe and learn. There is much looping and repetition. The key is to understand and develop the right probes for each task and then to be changed by the activity. To be changed is not simply to be internally changed — to have new ideas, it is to change your habits, practices, techniques, tools, taskspace, environment. There needs to be a co-emergent and co-evolutionary dialog between probing and the whole of what you are up to.

This is why innovation is an adventure — the destination and the territory do not exist before you set off.

task one

engage

"as we begin so shall we go"

a. n. whitehead

ENGAGE

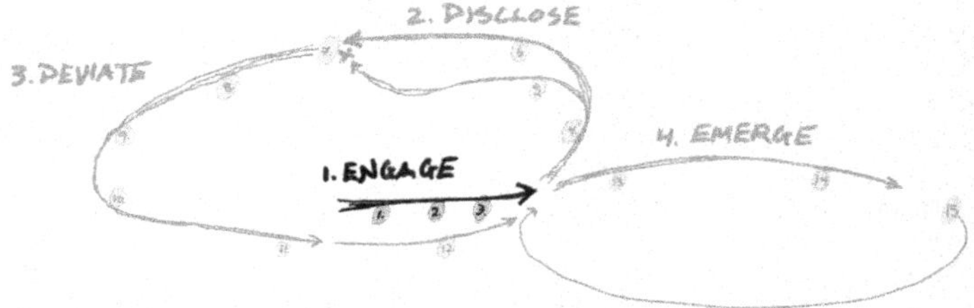

Beginning of the Innovation journey — this is the start of the adventure. On to the first task: Engage

Engagement is about being open to what can affect you. It is about being open to change, being open to the world and forces beyond what you know or might even comprehend. Innovation is not about imposing your vision upon the world. Innovation is about going beyond the known — it is about imagining that a new and totally unique way of being is possible.

To engage is fundamental to everything. There is nothing that is not always fully and totally the outcome of engagement. Emergence, systems design, probing, affordances, and exaptives — only come out from the middle of considered and deeply engaged action. Without doing and engaging nothing new can happen — only the old can reinforce itself. Everything is interdependent, emerges in action, and is the outcome of a web of complex forces. Thus innovation begins in the middle, and returns to the middle.

Too often we forget this, too often we have been taught otherwise. Many of our innovation models highlight the opposite: reflect, brainstorm, develop a plan or solution divorced from the world and others while sequestered in an office or studio. For perplexing reasons it is imagined that most of what matters can be treated separately from a real entanglement with history, community, and the environment.

Engagement is about others, it is about community — both human communities and non-human communities. All innovation design work is collective and collaborative. When we begin the design process we are making a shared space of possibility — a type of "commons", with others. This "proto-commons" is what will sustain and nurture the design process. Ideally one of the lasting outcomes of great design is the production of a new form of commons that allows new modes of being alive to flourish collectively (this is critical to genuine worldmaking).

Engage is also about the unintended — be on the lookout for the odd — It is important to always keep one eye focused on exaptive possibilities, even at this early stage in the process.

While it is OK, and even important, at the beginning of the process to believe you have a great idea that does something meaningful — don't confuse this "solution" with the "problem". And just as importantly don't confuse this "problem" with reality. Innovation requires, ironically, you to step back, reconsider the "problem" or question, and open yourself to what is beyond the known. Real innovation begins when you let go of existing solutions *and problems*, and believe that new problems and new worlds are possible. The philosopher Gilles Deleuze says it well "A solution always has the truth it deserves according to the problem to which it is a response."

Engage involves "making to put aside": we often see many innovators — especially entrepreneurs who start the innovation journey with a clear product idea that they believe is perfect and will change the world. There is not much more to say at this point that we haven't already said about how innovation is never a linear process, or the innovation paradox and the problem with ideas. If you have a realizable concept — make it. Make it to grow with it and through it to something else, welcome what comes next. We call this part of the task of Engage "making to put aside".

Slow down, become deeply curious, have an idea and

join the world — and then be moved and changed. Engage in the issue, see what others do, see what matters to others, collaborate fully. And while we call Engage a phase of the design process it is also something that you never stop doing — it will just take on differing forms as you move through the Innovation Design Process. We break the Engage phase down into three seemingly distinct stages: Opening & Grounding, Pattern Recognition, and Attuning and Gathering — while in reality it is best to blur these into one larger activity of initial engagement.

Remember, the great illusion is that we can have a view from nowhere. Design and innovation cannot afford this illusion — for it leads to many of the common problems we are faced with daily: things that solve nothing and make matters worse, or things that only made sense in the studio of the designer.

Probe, play, learn with and through the body. Remember that most things cannot be put in words. Be unruly. Engage immersively and transformatively in this great adventure.

SELF PREPARATION FOR IMMERSIVE ENGAGEMENT

BEFORE YOU BEGIN

Each task of Innovation requires a different mindset and approach. It is important to prepare yourself so as to be fully present in a manner that is most conducive to the goals of each phase. Here are our suggestions:

- Find collaborators and build/become part of a larger community
- Engage — fully and transformatively
- Be willing to be changed by whom you meet and what you do
- Be a participant and a good observer
- Suspend judgment
- See your biases, assumptions, and habits and bring them to light
- Be open-minded
- Learn and be changed
- Let go of your solutions and "solution thinking"
- Don't speak/assume others position
- Be willing to learn from others and the process
- Accept your ideas might be of limited value
- Embrace uncertainty & indeterminacy
- Work with others with whom you have nothing in common
- Surrender to process
- Care for your tools, practices and systems -- they are also your partners
- Develop a team: Bring those you meet into this process as part of your team for all of the phases of Innovation Design

- Understand that this is one step in a process and that you do not need to jump ahead or stay back -- Engage — participate — be subsumed — become other — make good notes — develop a team
- Be both of and alien to what you engage
- Be on the lookout for the unintended
- Build networks

TASK: ENGAGE

PRACTICE: 1. OPENING AND GROUNDING

OVERVIEW

At the beginning of any creative project you need to define a starting point. This is your initial idea or hunch which relates to a direct "problem" or "issue".

Once you have defined your starting point, take a moment, describe and draw it as best you can. It is useful that you have an idea that you are passionate about, but it does not need to be a great or perfect idea — this is, after all, simply the beginning.

Once you have this: PAUSE. This is only the starting point. The goal is *not to immediately begin perfecting this idea*. To do that would be to skip over the whole process of innovation.

At this moment what innovation requires of you is that you *slow down and put your idea/solution aside* — for solutions are like answers to existing questions, and innovation requires that we become curious about the possibility of new questions, new approaches and wholly new worlds.

Paradoxically, the goal at the beginning of a creative project *is not to be creative*, but to *engage* and understand the issue and the problem — really to take a more expansive view on things in general. How does one do this? Emersion. You settle into the territory, learn, find collaborators, and are changed by engagement.

Beginning with an initial concept/solution is important because it locates you and allows you to launch into developing an immersive understanding of what is going on. Innovation begins humbly by not making huge generalizations and assumptions but by deeply engaging with people, communities and everything that makes up your area of interest. Join them, learn from them, and experimentally become one of them.

Engage is also where we begin to get hints towards unintended capacities and affordances — be on the lookout for these and keep track of these as they surface. These will often be in the vicinity of accidents, errors, minor failures, jokes, wisecracks, asides, puns, tangential forays, etc.

Don't jump to solving anything, or creating something magical — that will come later, slow down and become of the world you are interested in. Take good notes, make good connections, find key sites and connect with potential collaborators.

Note: Often people focus far too much energy on perfecting the initial idea or having an astonishing initial idea — *where one starts is far less important than how one proceeds.* We like to quote the great innovator Sister Corita Kent:

"Begin Anywhere"

PROBES (questions/activities):

1. Area of Interest: What is your starting area of interest? Describe, take time to articulate fully.

- What are all the different ways you could participate in this area? List and then develop experimental ways to engage.
- As your thoughts become clear, connect with others to get their sense of this area of interest.
- Get a feel for the breadth and depth of this general area of interest.

2. Problem: Is your starting point something you wish to avoid or a problem to solve?? Describe the problem and the reasons for it being a problem.

- Take some time to re-experience this problem first hand. Be immersive. Record thoughts on the experience. Draw. Diagraming is helpful.

3. Making: Do you have an initial concept which you wish to make?

- Describe
- Could you draw some part of this? Draw
- Can you make this? Make (quickly, as best you can. Now use it and have others use it). Keep track of this activity.

4. Question & Issue: What is the immediate and direct issue/question your concept or your area of interest engages?

5. Assemblage: What is the assemblage that surrounds, supports and to some degree defines your concept or area of interest?

6. Unintended Affordances: What unintended possibilities are already emerging? List these & connect to *Practice #7 Probing toward the unintended.*

TASK: ENGAGE

PRACTICE: 2. ATTUNING & GATHERING

OVERVIEW

You are building upon the activities and insights that are developing from the practice of Opening and Grounding. Now you are turning outward from your perspective to that of others.

In this practice of attunement — you are connecting to the broader tacit and implicit feel of your area of interest. This happens through immersive engagement with others in the mundane practices of living from the perspective of your general area of interest. You will need to decide on a location(s) and a community(ies) with which to connect.

- Cultivate care and build lasting friendships. Be changed (already) by those you meet and what you and they do together.
- Sensing and probing context and history from a subjective point of view
- A type of highly participatory immersive anthropology.
- Community building — building a future community — the community still to come
- Proto-commons building
- Wandering further afield — following some of the unintended affordances
- What are people doing? What are their concerns? What is their world?

PROBES (QUESTIONS/ACTIVITIES)

7. Doing: What are people doing? Participate in a deep, embodied and enactive manner. As you become attuned to the rhythms (take your time), ask questions (but be equally attentive to the unspoken):

- Why are things done this way?
- What makes something well done or beautiful?
- Where does curiosity most often surface?
- Take note of the contexts of horror, dread, disgust and perplexity — how do they come into play in the general area of interest?
- Why are these things being used?
- What makes them so important/work so well?
- Have different practices been used in the past?
- Are you also using these things/processes to do other quite different things?
- What else is going on? Are there other interesting things happening that are worth following in adjacent spaces? (Go on a journey with your collaborators and partners into these spaces and activities).
- Partnering (capacity building) — forming collectives
- Sensing context and history
- Other questions/practices to consider?

8. Concerns: What are their concerns? Go deep with these questions — beyond the obvious

- What are people's deeper questions, concerns, purpose?
- Why does this area/activity really matter?

9. Summary & Conclusions: Review collectively what you have and draw conclusions in regards to your larger area of interest.

TASK: ENGAGE

PRACTICE: 3. PATTERN RECOGNITION

OVERVIEW

This is the beginning of your shift from Engagement to Analysis. You are going from your deep immersive engagement with an area of interest to begin to develop a more general and abstract understanding of what is going on in your area of interest.

As you fill out this worksheet look back at your notes from ENGAGEMENT, these will help you immensely. This analysis begins by Seeing Patterns (this stage), and moves onto uncovering problems, approaches, paradigms and worlds in the next stage. This is a process of moving from being focused on a solution (your initial idea) to uncovering the deeper issues that this solution is engaged in. We call this "falling in love with the concern, and not the solution."

Everything has a history — a before, an elsewhere, and an after.

Begin by framing the problem that your idea "answers". Then the processes of zooming out can begin: you will sequentially answer questions to get at the big picture:

- What is the domain?
- What is its underlying purpose?
- What is its history?
- What are the trends shaping it?
- What are the big patterns that keep repeating?
- What is the matter of concern?

Note: Answering these questions requires research — both questioning users, observing what is really going on, and digging into scholarship. As such it is done collaboratively with both members of the community affected by the question/issue and those that can offer differing forms of insight (anthropologists, sociologists, philosophers, historians, etc.).

PROBES (questions/activities):

10. Domain: An area or region. This is a question about context. You are trying to situate your idea/interest in a larger context. Additionally, you are taking a broad view to see what are all the other things that also are part of this domain.

- What domain is it in?
- How would you define this larger field?
- Articulate the features, logics, goals and oppositions within and across this domain
- Diagram the relation of parts in the domain
- What is adjacent to this domain? Are there unintended possibilities here? List these & connect to Section 7 (probing toward the unintended)

11. What Exists: List everything that looks like or functions like or leads to the same outcome. This is a critical step — do not do this in a cursory manner — especially if you think your design /idea/approach is exceptionally unique, for it is in this stage that you will be quickly able to see if it is or not. Most often our ideas are not as unique as we at first might imagine. If it is not as unique as hoped, don't worry, you will get there — the process will take us to truly novel outcomes. Doing this step well allows us to block what exists and push the project into genuine novelty.

- What else exists?
- Categorize into distinct groups based upon (1) physical similarities and (2) similarities in method. Diagram each. Use color to help differentiate components.
- List everything that currently exists and solves the same issue/question differently

12. Approaches: How would you define the underlying approach(s) to this domain?

- What are the big patterns that repeat? Diagram & try and locate your project within this diagram

13. Purpose: What is the larger purpose of this domain?

- Why are things done this way?
- What makes something well done or beautiful in this

domain?

- Why are these things being used (vs others)?
- What is important?

14. History: When did the current approach to your area of interest begin?

- How did it come about?
- What was done prior?
- Where does this approach not exist? Why?

15. Emerging Trends & Forces: Innovation and creativity do not exist in a vacuum, things are constantly shifting both on the micro and macro levels. Trends are the emergence of the new macro forces that have the potential to shift the entire logic of a field or culture. Research trends relevant to the larger area.

- In your area of interest:
- What is emerging?
- What is changing?
- What is stable in your area?

End of Engage task — But not the end of this process of engagement.

- Take time to review, present and discuss.
- Organize and summarize what has emerged.
- Pay particular attention to how things have already shifted, and what unintended capacities and affordances are surfacing.
- Continue to ground yourself in the context, communities, and commons.
- Move forward collaboratively and experimentally.
- Return to these questions, activities and your conclusions as you move through the tasks of innovation.
- What you have learned in these three sub-phases or stages of Engage that will ground what you do next.
- Additionally, engagement — doing is fundamental to all and any innovation activity. *Stay deeply engaged.*

task two

disclose

"there is absolutely no inevitability as long as there is a willingness to comtemplate what is happening"

m. mcluhan

DISCLOSURE

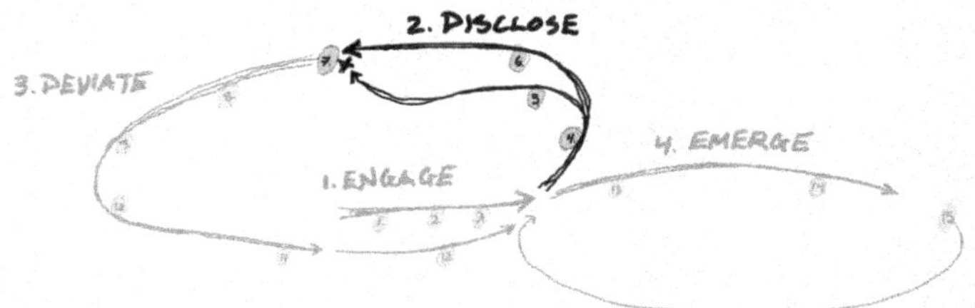

Disclosure is to go beyond the immediate understanding of things. Why do this? It is not simply for the sake of knowledge. Disclosure allows one to understand and engage with the more fundamental logic of any situation, practice, object or concept. A richer understanding of any situation allows us to grasp what is really going on and come to a more strategic and creative response.

Disclosure begins from the realization that things don't happen on their own, the ideas we have and the questions we ask along with the solutions we propose are based in more general assumptions, frameworks, habits, patterns, and ways of being alive. If we do not disclose these logics we tend to unknowingly repeat these patterns, or miss how profound an object or a concept might be. If creativity involves not repeating — then it involves not repeating the more general logics. In this manner creativity requires a rich and nuanced critical approach to the given

Disclosure can be used in two ways for creativity:

First, to discover novel assumptions, frameworks and ways of being in new experimental objects and processes (see inner dashed line in diagram). Too often we make things to solve problems, without considering how radically novel something might be (worldblindness). This leads us to miss the true novelty and potential of what we are doing. Taking time to disclose the deeper and more far reaching novelty of any innovation is critical to both grasping and participating in its impact.

The second goal of disclosing what is really going on is to prepare for disruptive innovation. Disruptive innovation requires that we "step out of the box" and this is only possible if we really know what "box" we are in. Disclosure does this. It is about discovering the patterns that keep repeating and leading to similar outcomes. Disclosure is part anthropology and part being a sleuth: what is going on and why? Patterns lead to approaches and approaches lead to paradigms and paradigms lead to worlds, and shifting worlds lead to a disruptive innovation. Much of this — the patterns, approaches, paradigms and worlds — is invisible, tacit and very difficult to disclose. Don't be put off by this, the difficulty is part of the pleasure of disclosure. Remember, this part of the creative process is about understanding, not proposing creative alternatives (that begins in the next phase: Deviate).

Disclosure also does something else: it allows you to begin to see alternative and unintended potentials that could be the beginning of novelty. Here it is critical to remind ourselves that all disruptive innovation involves the utilization of some unintended potential. We see this in literally all major innovations: from bird wings, eyes, transistors, electricity, penicillin, the internet, the wheel — and on and on... The hard part of innovation is that it is exceedingly difficult to notice anything new as being new — we tend to see novelty as either a mistake or as something we already understand — if we notice it at all. Seeing, or better yet sensing the unintended requires the willingness to be "stupid" to put aside what we know and how we know and speculate, test, play, experiment, and putter. Ultimately it requires of us a willingness to "follow" and not lead. We follow unintended "things" without knowing where they will lead and in the process we let them change us and our world.

Thus we need to do two quite distinct and even opposite things: know deeply and follow unknowingly. This is no easy task: to know and not-know simultaneously. Go easy on yourself. Laugh a lot. Stay seriously playful.

This is why our diagram splits in two (see above). Branch #1 helps you find which box you are in, and Branch #2 helps you find unintended potentials. Remember: Disclosing well — getting to the level of revealing a world allows one to really deviate and innovate a new world.

SELF PREPARATION OF DISCLOSING

BEFORE YOU BEGIN

Each task of Innovation requires a different mindset and approach. It is important to prepare yourself so as to be fully present in a manner that is most conducive to the goals of each phase. Here are our suggestions:

Your mindset and approach needs to shift as you move from Engage to Disclose. Disclose can seem like it is all about our normal critical practices of uncovering, but it is the most paradoxical and even schizophrenic of the phases because it asks us to do two quite opposite things: (1) Disclose underlying patterns of organizing, behaving, and thinking as well as (2) to be crow-like and experimentally disclose unintended possibilities. Thus your mindset must become "critical-creative".

1. CRITICAL DISCLOSURE:

- Fall in love with the issue and not the solution
- Pause, slow down and go back — engage more
- Opening up to the field of possibilities
- Getting settled into the larger problem and what grounds it
- Interrogating and researching systems deeply
- Seeing patterns, abstract gestures, and basic operations
- Finding histories and historical ruptures
- Noticing and critically following trends
- Uncovering and abstracting
- Generalizing

2. EXAPTIVE DISCLOSURE:

- Be like a Crow (experiment beyond purpose)
- Play, putter, tinker, make, use, do
- Using without considering purpose
- Jumping fields
- Search for distant and tangential similarities (broad research)
- Welcome difference
- Attune yourself away for mental reflection and towards embodied sensing of differences
- Recognize, welcome and follow your feelings of perplexity, wonder, horror, embarrassment, and disgust -- these are emotional harbingers of difference
- Be comfortable with being unsettled
- Don't force the ambiguous and nebulous to resolve themselves
- Laugh a lot
- Follow and do not lead

TASK: DISCLOSE

ACTIVITY: 4. DEFINING

OVERVIEW

At this point in your innovation journey it is critical to begin to separate and distinguish between the issue (the general area of interest) and what underpins it: a larger matter of concern. Why? Separating the two allows you to remove yourself from a pre-given path (the area of interest) that generates a limited field of possible problems, questions and solutions. Locating yourself in a bigger and more abstract space (the matter of concern) will allow you to co-emerge and co-evolve with a new path and develop an alternative world.

An example is helpful: you begin with a problem: *the chairs you are sitting on lead to serious back problems*. You define your area of interest: *how we "sit" to engage with work related tasks* (and how we might reinvent this). And after engaging with this in a myriad of manners you can now define your matter of concern to be: *how we connect our bodies to the environment*.

The first thing to note with our example — neither the area of interest nor the matter of concern are objective — you are making a strategic decision to frame things one way or another based upon an emerging sensibility and perspective. This can change — and often there is a need to test out multiple distinct ways of framing both your area of interest and your matter of concern.

For example, we could have defined our area of interest: *back health*, and our matter of concern: *the spine and gravity*. This would lead to a very different innovation journey. Consequently it is important to generate multiple different versions of each — especially your matter of concern.

Defining a "Matter of Concern": When we use this term the word "concern" often throws people — what are we so concerned about? It often gets understood as a "concern" that a teacher might have for a failing student. We are using in the way the Quakers used this word: a concern is something we are deeply engaged with, profoundly curious about, and comes to animate all of our activities. It is most definitely not a negative term — not a worry. Rather than worry, we should hear care, engagement and curiosity in this term "concern."

Solutions are answers to questions, and questions are ways of concretely approaching a problem. A Matter of Concern is the general area of interest of a problem or question. A Matter of Concern helps us go from the specific to the general and in doing so recognize that not only are there many ways to solve a problem — there are many, many ways to approach things. The power of getting to a general matter of concern is that we are freed up to see that not only are there many solutions and questions, but that there are many approaches. This begins to open us up to new emergent spaces of invention and novelty.

What is important to keep in mind when defining a Matter of Concern is:

- It needs to be abstract
- To the degree it can, it needs to distinguish itself from our general ontology and world.
- It cannot be so abstract that it is meaningless (has no purchase on reality)
- It should feel generative.
- This is an unruly creative moment
- Your "definition" will become a creative agent in the process (love it)
- You can keep tweaking and transforming this
- Don't forget what your matter of concern is as you move forward

PROBES (questions/activities):

16. Matter of concern: What is the underlying "concern" that the larger domain of your issue/question/solution deals with?

- Name this
- Define this as carefully as possible. Be rigorous. Develop your answer from real engagement. Don't rush through this. Usually this is an inquiry into the core values of a culture.

17. A Way of Life: How does this "matter of concern" tie to a way of life?

18. Alternative Approaches: What totally different approaches exist to your matter of concern that might be found in other cultures or historic moments?

- Research (did you already come across some during the task of Engage?
- Define
- Connect: If possible connect as directly as possible with these. Go there. Read ethnographies. Meet people. Participate. Watch movies, etc.

20. Reconsideration: Are there other ways to define your matter of concern?

- List these
- What are the speculative consequences of each?
- Do you feel you have the "right" Matter of Concern?
- Experiment, test and revise till you feel satisfied

TASK: DISCLOSE

ACTIVITY: 5. UNCOVERING (Immanent Paradigms & Worlds)

OVERVIEW

This is the final analytical stage prior to beginning to creatively deviate from what is currently done.

It is only if this stage is done effectively that you will understand well enough the "box" that you are in — such that you can effectively "block" it, and develop a truly different mode of being alive.

Disclosing the "box" that you are in is an activity of ontological world disclosure.

To do this you are looking to understand three things:

1. What is the current approach that is being used?
2. What is the ethos/logic that underlies this approach?
3. What is the world that all of this fits into?

Once you understand these then in the next phase, they can be "blocked" — which will push your project into a novel and experimental terrain of possibility (the third phase: Deviate). Thus it is critical that you successfully uncover the deep logic of your area of interest: deviation is relying upon it!

To do this next section well it is critical to grasp four key concepts:

Approach: there is always a basic approach that is being taken towards an issue. This can usually be stated very simply. For example, a bar of soap has a basic approach (framework) to the question of hygiene that is "cleaning involves removing". Thus one could say that soap operates within a "cleaning = separating + removing" approach to health.

Assemblage: Nothing works alone. The assemblage is the holistic but open set of things, practices, environments, laws etc.

Ethos: underlying any approach is a set of unspoken assumptions, values, goals and habits. These need to be brought to light so that they can be put aside (via blocking).

World/Paradigm: Behind and supporting an ethos and the approach is a world or a paradigm. A paradigm is the invisible, assumed, unthought, habitual *concepts, tools and practices* that co-shape us and our most basic outlook. The paradigm could be thought of as the "mindset." Some paradigm always underlies how we understand, recognize and interact with the world. In essence: the world we have available to us because of our mode of being in the world (paradigm).

Paradigms, while complex and having many supporting components, can be stated simply. For example the "hygiene paradigm" of our bar of soap assumes that reality can be divided up into two basic categories: clean & dirty (pure & impure), and that the goal of life is to manage these (keep them apart). Paradigms always affect more than one field or issue. Again, looking at the hygiene paradigm we can see that this shapes how immigration issues, religious matters, and ecological issues are approached.

From an understanding of the approach and paradigm that lies behind and supports an idea or practice or product we can then define the "world" that this "thing" inhabits. The concept of "world" here can be understood as being synonymous with "culture" or "ontology".

Continuing our soap example, we can now ask: what is the world of "hygiene people"? What do they care about? How do they approach things? How do all the differing parts of their world fit together?

Immanence: the logic is not separate from its instantiation in practices, environments and things.

By uncovering specifically how we are always part of an assumed implicit world we can understand that our "Matter of Concern" might transcend our world and allow us a way to leave one paradigm and invent and enter into a new paradigm/world.

For innovation, defining these four concepts is critical. This next section asks you to do this. It will require research — going to the books, talking to experts, etc. These are not things one understands easily or all at once. It will take research, testing and debate.

Work on one question at a time. Write in pencil, make lots of notes, try out differing answers. Finish each question before moving onto the next.

PROBES (questions/activities):

21. Form: What is the basic underlying form (shape). Describe and make an annotated drawing. Be abstract.

- What is the general material condition? Describe.
- How would you categorize (and even diagram) the basic material assemblage (organized system) that this is part of? Describe and draw/diagram

22. Approach: What is the framework your concept uses to approach its area of interest?

23. World: What is the implicit logic behind this approach/framework. Articulate the habits, tools, thought patterns and practices.

- Ethos: Describe the ethos, general unspoken culture, and general values that are a critical part of this world.

NOTE: Getting these three questions right is critical to everything that follows. Understanding the world that you are in...

Do not move forward to the next task (Deviate) without having really dug into these questions and fully answered them in a way that brings to light as much of the deep implicit nature of a world as possible.

TASK: DISCLOSE

ACTIVITY: 6. EXPLORATION (towards the unintended)

PROBING TOWARDS UNINTENDED POTENTIALS

OVERVIEW

There is one last stage prior to moving on to the next phase of Deviation. This is a deeply rewarding and experimental stage in which you will probe to uncover unintended potentials.

All disruptive innovations utilize some unintended potential that is found in things, processes or systems. This can be quite simply done by the moving of something from one domain to another (while perhaps changing scale, materials and purpose). There are countless examples of this: Viagra began as a heart medicine; the Wright Brothers transposed hip steering from bikes to kites; Dinosaurs became birds in part by utilizing "wings" that evolved to keep eggs warm for the purpose of falling out of trees safely. The other way unintended purposes emerge is by finding something without purpose and utilizing it to develop new forms of purpose.

The unintended is all around us and we utilize it constantly: when we don't have a rolling pin we use a wine bottle. And in doing so we might discover additional possibilities — perhaps a one-handed rolling pin (the wine bottle) is "better" at certain things? Other examples: the empty swimming pool was the first skateboarding bowl, Velcro was discovered by looking at seeds stuck in socks. This list is literally endless and encompasses all innovation.

It is worth returning to our earlier list of the differing forms of the unintended:

- Intentional Components with unintended but existing effects
- Intentional Components that no longer have a use
- Unintentional Components that are physical by-products
- Unintentional Components that are chance by-products

- Unintentional Components working in category
- Unintentional *Components working across category*

Begin by reviewing the answers and research you have already done.

Finding unintended possibilities is a key part of Disclosure. It allows us a starting place as we move forward to disrupt the existing and the known.

This process is counterintuitive, illogical, and disorienting to many — for we are trained to be idea generators and to trust in what can be known via concepts. But as we explained in the introduction the genuinely new is at first wholly unconceptualizable and is available to us only in action via vague hunches.

Take your time. Test things — start with your ideas and objects: play and tinker with them: what unintended potentials do they have? Are there other things in the world related to these potentials? Play. Mess around. Break things. Use things in entirely strange and nonsensical ways — invent new practices and habits. Research how others might be approaching things (don't limit yourself to our culture, this historical moment or any specific facts — speculate far and wide).

Ultimately the unintended possibilities that you discover/co-create *do not have to be complex*. In fact some of the most profound were astonishingly simple: Jackson Pollock changed art by embracing and following the unintended power of the paint drip. It is simply the beginning of differing. They will develop and get complex later. The key is to discover as many as possible, so that you can select the most promising. Make notes as you collect possibilities. List these and sketch their unique use.

Remember:

EXAPTIVE DISCLOSURE:

- Be like a Crow (experiment beyond purpose)
- Play, putter, tinker, make, use, do
- Using without considering purpose
- Jumping fields
- Search for distant and tangential similarities (broad research)
- Welcome difference
- Attune yourself away for mental reflection and towards embodied sensing of differences
- Recognize, welcome and follow your feelings of perplexity, wonder, horror, embarrassment, and disgust -- these are emotional harbingers of difference
- Be comfortable with being unsettled
- Don't force the ambiguous and nebulous to resolve themselves
- Laugh a lot
- Follow and do not lead

PROBES (questions/activities):

24: Unintended Potentials - Project: Return to your project and all the notes you have made. List and describe all of the unintended possibilities that emerged during this early research.

25. Unintended Potentials - Process: Return to your project and all the notes you have made. List and describe all of the unintended possibilities that emerged during this early research.

26. Unintended Potentials - From Elsewhere: Return to your notes on exaptive possibilities that you have been making in parallel to this process. Are there any hints of unintended potentials in other fields? Can you poach a thing, or a process from elsewhere and repurpose it in some potentially novel manner? Do other creatures fulfil your matter of concern in a wholly different manner? Speculate and research broadly. Note: much of biomimicry follows from this question.

27. Synthesize and Diagram: Diagram the relations between the various unintended potentials from previous questions. Use the Exaptive/Adaptive Diagram as a rough template. Collectively speculate on what you have: make note of the "most novel" (a judgement call) connections and salient outliers. Highlight all of the most interesting, odd and novel potentials. Carry this over into the summary below.

28. Summarize Disclosure: Work with your expanding community to synthesize and summarize the previous two task around these three topics:

- Matter of Concern
- World
- Unintended Possibilities

task three

deviate

"There is nothing new under the sun, but there are new suns."

o. e. butler

DEVIATE

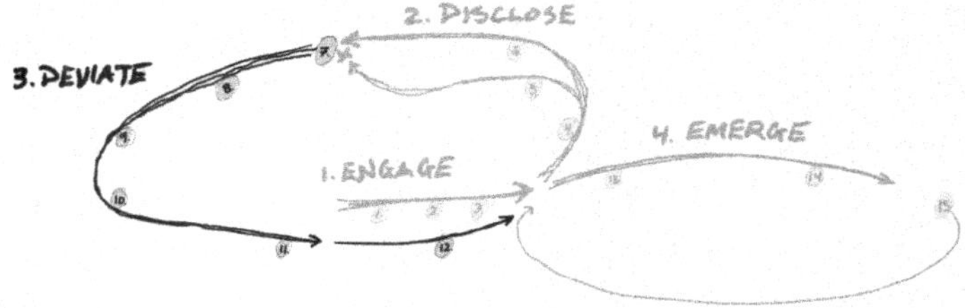

Congratulations! You have successfully moved through the second task of innovation. You have disclosed a historical mode of being-in-the-world (a world) and its unintended potentials. Now you are ready to really get creative and experimental. In this task you will be deviating from the world you disclosed so as to evolve a novel world. This is done by a two part experimental process of (1) blocking, and (2) following unintended consequences.

The goal of this process of deviation is to develop a novel world. A disruptive innovation leaves one world behind, and fosters the emergence of a new and novel world. Deviation is challenging precisely because of this — you are in a sense returning to zero. You are blocking and putting behind you the ways that things have been done, and you are setting off on an aberrant journey in which the hope is that a qualitatively new way of being emerges. Here you enter an unknowable journey — you are, as the poet Antonio Machado says, "laying down a path in walking". Your actions make the path into the future in real time.

Again, remember, you are not trying to come up with a new "product" or outcome (solution) just yet. In the final phase (Emerge) you will develop an outcome, a "product" if you will. Products are types of solutions. Solutions are answers to questions and questions are the outcome of a worldview. Thus the first thing that needs to be done is to develop a new and novel worldview.

In this phase you are developing a novel world view via refusing the framework you have disclosed and experimentally following the most promising unintended potentials in a way that lets a world emerge.

Once you have a novel world articulated, there is still one more task to accomplish in this phase and that is "mapping and relocating." A novel world by itself means little — the real question is how can this world and its worldview make a transformative impact on our current reality? We do this by mapping how they could meet, and relocating our focus of interest and experimentation to an area that seems most promising.

Review the material earlier in the book on exaptation to help you prepare for these experiments.

A word of caution and promise: this phase is by far the most challenging: knowledge and expertise are of little help — everything will become vague, nebulous and uncertain. There will be dead-ends and irresolvable paradoxes. There will be many frustrating moments when you simply fall back into the known. You will doubt yourself and what you are doing. It will make little sense when you attempt to explain things to outsiders. Have faith, trust the process and most of all trust your experiments — they will lead somewhere.

SELF PREPARATION FOR DEVIATING

BEFORE YOU BEGIN

Each task of Innovation requires a different mindset and approach. It is important to prepare yourself so as to be fully present in a manner that is most conducive to the goals of each phase. Here are our suggestions for Deviation:

Deviating is the most experimental, open and "creative" of the phases. Because of this it draws upon some of the same skills, and mental models that you needed to use during the second half of Disclose. Now you really need to push these habits even further.

- Trust the process
- Take blocking and blockages seriously
- Be open to whatever comes next — welcome whatever comes next
- Welcome difference
- Attune yourself away from mental reflection and towards embodied sensing of differences
- Recognize, welcome and follow your feelings of perplexity, wonder, horror, embarrassment, and disgust -- these are emotional harbingers of difference
- Be comfortable with being unsettled
- Don't force the ambiguous and nebulous to resolve themselves
- Play, putter, tinker, make, use, do
- Be like a crow
- Stick with the difficulty
- Laugh a lot
- Follow and do not lead
- Let events, objects and practices speak
- Make new tools, develop new habits, use new words

TASK: DEVIATE

ACTIVITY: 7. ENTERING (defining the scope)

OVERVIEW

This is where the radically new begins. This happens via two powerful and simple operations: 1. you refuse to do what has already been done, this act we call "blocking"; and 2. you develop a new starting point based upon unintended consequences and you "follow" this away from the old and towards the new. This can be understood as a very simple formula: "Block X and Follow Y" (where X is the old logic and Y is something unintended).

1. Blocking is a critical act for creativity. All too often we imagine that creativity is about being free of all rules, this is partially true — you do want to put aside the existing rules, but the real key is to then *develop new alternative rules*. These new rules are negative (don't do what has been done) and because of this are paradoxically *enabling and catalytic*. Blocking is an enabling constraint.

Blocking relies on knowing what to block. How do you know what to block? It is what you disclosed about how things work on a deep structural level during the previous sections of Disclosure. Begin by reviewing your Disclosure work: did you really uncover the deep logic of the existing paradigm of your matter of concern? Did you fully uncover a rich and diverse set of unintended possibilities? Only when you feel confident in your answers to these questions should you proceed to this section.

Blocking is not an all or nothing operation — there is great flexibility and nuance in it. With blocking you are first deciding how deep you want to block: the more elements and the deeper you block the more novel the outcome will be. If you block simple things you will get a change-in-degree. It is only when you block more and deeper elements that you will get a change-in-kind. This is up to you.

The key in blocking is to consciously remember at every moment after this decision: *you cannot have anything to do with what you have blocked.* It needs to be a complete break. Keep track of what you have written and treat it like a contract, check what you do against it and make sure you follow it.

Remember: *it is a speculative and empowering contract:* if it leads to nothing interesting simply return to this section and change what you block and what you follow.

2. Following & Experimenting: Once you have established a block, you can now begin to deviate. Since you have blocked the standard approaches you can no longer proceed in a forward manner with your design. You will need to find a new beginning place within your world of unintended possibilities. This is what we are calling "following & experimenting" — you are following alternative (unintended) pathways & potentials and pushing them further via experiments.

Carefully answer the questions below and treat them like a starting place — your experiments in the next stage will take you further afield via a series of multiple sideways moves — don't get fixated on where you started — allow things to evolve and change (just remember not to slip back into what you have blocked) and draw from this.

Remember two things:

1. That these are hunches and speculations at this point. You need to put something down and try something out to see where it takes you. You cannot know in advance if it will lead anywhere. So the best policy is to trust the process and see where it takes you.

2. At this stage you are not trying to develop a novel solution to anything. These experiments are probes into the unknown with the goal of co-evolving and co-emerging with a novel world/paradigm.

PROBES (questions/activities):

Treat these two questions as a type of experimental "contract": for the length of the experiment you will abide by the following conditions of blocking and following.

In an ideal world you can set up multiple tests of different blockings and followings that would connect to differing definitions of the Area of Interest and the Matter of Concern.

Be speculative and inventive in developing from this "contract". Always go back and rethink both what you could block (the ontological world) and what you could follow (sense new possible unintended capacities to engage).

29. Blocking:

- What is the basic form to be blocked?
- What is the basic logic of materiality to be blocked?
- What is the underlying approach (or aspect of an approach) to be blocked?
- What world — or aspect of a world is being blocked?

30. Following: List the most promising (a speculative judgement call) unintended:

- Functions
- Processes
- Purposes

TASK: DEVIATE

ACTIVITY: 8. EXPERIMENTING

OVERVIEW

Now it is time to experiment. The goal of this experiment is to develop a new approach to your general area of interest. It is really important to understand this:

You are not trying in this phase to develop anything like a product, and in this activity all you are working on is developing a new approach.

You can think of this idea of "an approach" like a "doorway" — it is just the beginning of a direction that when opened might lead to a new terrain and ideally — a new paradigm.

This phase is really difficult. There is no roadmap to the new — if there was it would not be new. It is easy to block things. Now you are creating what you do not know. You will have to rely on intuitions and hunches. Not everything you develop will lead anywhere, that's OK. Trust your collaborators. Bring in outsiders. Try out lots of things. Don't judge if things are "good" or "bad" (that will come later), right now just evaluate if they are different.

Here are some techniques we use to get started in probing experiments:

- Take what you blocked, what is its opposite? Are there existing things like this in existence? In nature? What are they?
- What exists outside of both what you blocked and it's opposite? What would it mean to use this as a starting point? Again, Are there existing things like this in existence? In nature? What are they?
- Apply the goal of your novel world to the actual form and logic of the novel world (make form and content match). For example: the goal of a knife is to cut — can you make a knife that cuts itself?
- Remember: it does not have to make sense, be realistic, you do not have to like it, nor is it a product.
- Make things, do things, test things — learn from making and doing.

RULES FOR EXPERIMENTATION

EXPERIMENT AND DISCOVER THE UNINTENDED IN ACTION

- Push the unintended further — increase or decrease size, value, scale
- Be experimental — value making-thinking over ideation-creation
- EXPERIMENT & CO-OPT THINGS FOR NEW PURPOSES
- Utilize the invisible & unintended
- Mix, hybridize, and mutate the unintended, the chance, the co-opted

GO SIDEWAYS RATHER THAN FORWARD

- Transpose the unintended and the co-opted into new fields and practices
- Ignore intended purpose(s)

EXPERIMENT IN A HOLISTIC MANNER

- Don't focus on one thing or scale work in a distributed and multi-scalar manner
- Develop mixes, hybrids, and mutations of the unintended, the chance, the co-opted

EXPERIMENTALLY FOLLOW ACROSS THRESHOLDS

- Follow, *perturbate, iterate and push things until thresholds are crossed and novelty emerges (a qualitative difference)
- Work in a distributed and multi-scalar manner

SPECULATE IN MAKING AT THE SCALE OF WORLDS

- In the midst of experimentation ask about the global ramifications of what you are doing as a total way of being-in-the-world
- Paradigmatically define your actions as novel frameworks and methodologies

**Perturbation: a deviation in a system caused by an outside force. To perturbate: verb — to act on a system to cause it to deviate*

PROBES (questions/activities):

You are developing and carrying out a series of iterative experiments that follow the Exaptive Design process.

NOTE: This process repeats and co-evolves until a novel threshold is sensed. We lay this out below as three iterations — but it could be hundreds... When that threshold is sensed, then and only then is it time to move onto the next Practice: Transversal Articulation

A Note on Diagrams: Key to an experimentation for the production of unintended possibilities is an understanding of how any "thing", say water in a glass, is simply the instantiation of something (in this case H2O) under the specific forces of variables (here pressure and temperature).

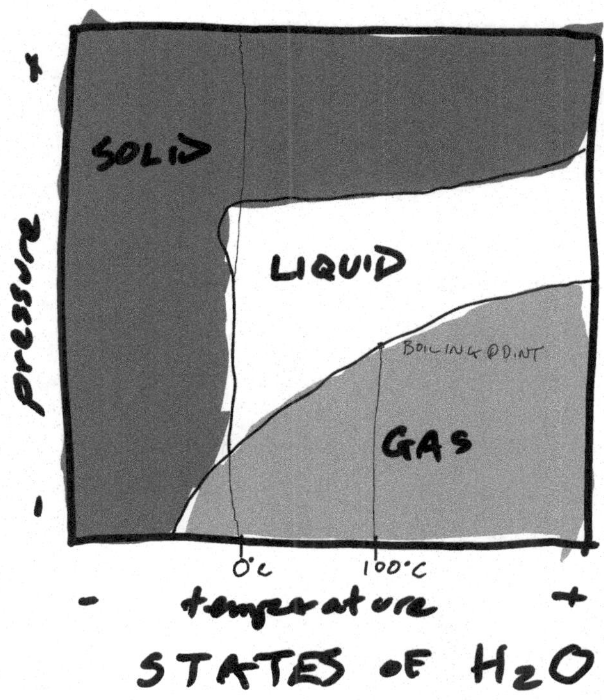

If you can understand that every "thing" or " event" around us is simply a particular instantiation of critical variables. And that these variables form an invisible but real *field of variation*. The diagram below of H2O is a very simple version of this.

Two things are key:

1. Once you know what the key variables are, you can move anywhere in this expanded field — you are not limited to experimenting with what is right in front of you. You move from seeing only the glass of water in front of you to seeing all the possibilities of liquids, gases and solids. A much larger area to explore.

2. You can change the underlying variables — then everything changes. A qualitatively new field of possibility emerges to be explored. How do you change the underlying variables? This is not simply a conceptual act: you need to change the assemblage or make a new assemblage.

In innovation there is always a relay between shifting assemblages, discovering immanent fields (via diagramming), exploring those fields and repeating this process iteratively towards the new.

The methods we use below all rely on this understanding and technique.

29. Experiment Iteration #1

Diagram: Layout a terrain to experiment in using an X, Y diagram. Define three highly distinct areas of interest. Develop an experimental approach for deeply engaging each.

Experiment #1: carry out and make meticulous notes

Experiment #2: carry out and make meticulous notes

Experiment #3: carry out and make meticulous notes

Synthesize: review all experiments — what is most interesting and novel? What suggests a new approach? What changes the underlying variables of your diagram in an interesting and different manner

30. Experiment Iteration #2

Review & Diagram: develop a new diagram based upon the previous round of experimentation. Layout a terrain to experiment in using an X, Y diagram. Define three highly distinct areas of interest. Develop an experimental approach for deeply engaging each.

Experiment #1: carry out and make meticulous notes

Experiment #2: carry out and make meticulous notes

Experiment #3: carry out and make meticulous notes

Synthesize: review all experiments — what is most interesting and novel? What suggests a new approach? What changes the underlying variables of your diagram in an interesting and different manner

31. Experiment Iteration #3

Review & Diagram: develop a new diagram based upon the previous round of experimentation. Layout a terrain to experiment in using an x,y diagram. Define three highly distinct areas of interest. Develop an experimental approach for deeply engaging each.

Experiment #1: carry out and make meticulous notes

Experiment #2: carry out and make meticulous notes

Experiment #3: carry out and make meticulous notes

Synthesize: review all experiments — what is most interesting and novel? What suggests a new approach? What changes the underlying variables of your diagram in an interesting and different manner. When you reach a point in these iterations that feels paradigmatically novel and truly interesting. Really develop this as a diagram, and an assemblage. This will begin the next activity.

TASK: DEVIATE

PRACTICE: 9. TRANSVERSAL ARTICULATION

Being able to sense and then successfully cross thresholds (between degree and kind) is critical to the development of a disruptive innovation. As the iterations of blocking and following develop the question is always is this a meaningful/relevant threshold? Is there something different here? How can this difference be sensed and stabilized?

This practice is less a neat step in the process than a form of constant awareness and curiosity.

Additionally it is a moment of articulation — turning — that folds one back into experimentation differently — AND it draws one out of this process to bend into the next practice of Worlding.

Ultimately this is the practice of being a threshold — a portal — a step between worlds, between paradigms. Between the old and the not yet existent new.

PROBES (questions/activities):

32. Articulate: Take what seems like a promising exaptation. Define it abstractly as a topological terrain composed of two variables. It might take a few speculations to get the "right" variable.

33. Diagram: Make a topological diagram of this exaptation using an X, Y diagram. Mark on it a set of distinct extreme points to explore. We usually recommend 5.

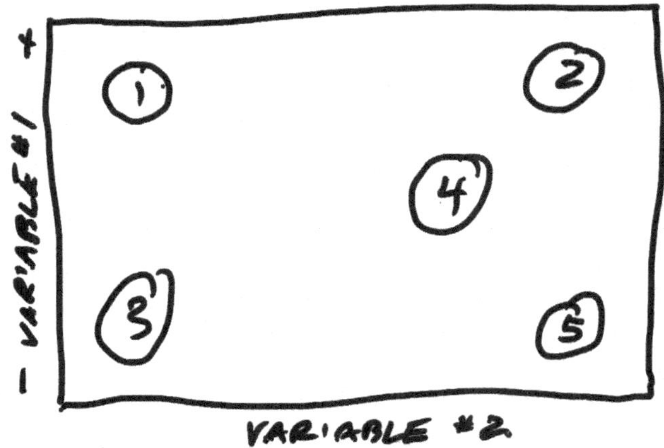

34. Speculate and experiment: Speculate what the conditions/world is like at each point. Define and describe each of these as a separate space. Develop a set of experiments to test, engage and ultimately expand this space. Learn form the unexpected and novel (exaptive) outcomes that happen in doing the actual experiments. Do not simply ideate this. That will be pointless.

35. Iterate: Start again with #32 and repeat a few times. At some point in this process the radical nature of your difference will be apparent. Trust this — however strange, and challenging it might be. Be prepared for the fact that in following it you will betray much of your past.

36: Rearticulate: transpose the novel emergent possible paradigm into the next practice:

TASK: DEVIATE

PRACTICE: 10. WORLDING

Speculative extrapolation

OVERVIEW

To develop a novel world is the heart of disruptive innovation. It is a speculative act of futurological making which has much in common with forms of fiction that project alternative histories and futures. The work of Ursula Le Guin, Kim Stanley Robinson, Octania E. Butler, Madeline Miller or Charlie Jane Anders are good examples of this speculative turn. This act of speculative world making is also found in the sciences: the works of Darwin, and Lynn Margulis are good examples. Here it's referred to as a paradigm change -- but the process is the same. What is critical at this stage is that you are proposing an alternative all-encompassing alternative approach to your matter of concern. Making a novel world is not to propose a new solution to an old problem -- it is to change the very ground rules entirely. The profound difficulty in this step is that novel worlds sound absurd and cannot be proven — they are genuinely projective speculations: this might be revolutionary, but then again it could lead to nothing. And in such a situation the tendency is to be swayed by criticism of the "devil's advocate" kind: that would never work! why would you ever want to think this way? It is important to keep these forms of criticism away (they are valuable — but only much later in the process, during the Emerge phase).

Take your most promising and different experiments and treat them like they are worlds. This is a speculative exercise. The next steps guide you through a process of turning a promising "portal" into a full fledged paradigm. The best way to approach this is to select a few of your most promising experiments and work through the questions.. It *is really important to answer the questions in the most radical manner possible* — by which we mean: you are concretely defining a world and there can be a tendency at this point to make it sound more "normal" and "reasonable" — but to do this is to lose your difference. *Keep your difference alive.*

The other thing to keep in mind as you complete this set of questions is that you are beginning to define a qualitatively different world. Keep it qualitatively different — don't evaluate it by the rules, logic, values and beauty that exist — it will have its own rules, logic, values and beauty.

Worlds, paradigms, and frameworks are best diagrammed and drawn out — words only go so far. We recommend making a (1) drawing of the world and (2) a diagram of the process that underlies your paradigm.

Sometimes it makes more sense to make a diagram of your world rather than a representational drawing. Either way, label and define all key components.

The diagram of the process is a type of flow chart. It will lay things out in a sequential manner.

Write a manifesto summarizing your values, purpose and logic. An itemized list is best. Start with the most general concepts and go to the most specific. Be clear and define terms that you are using in a unique manner.

Note: don't confuse your personal beliefs with those of your innovation. Perhaps they do overlap, but first and foremost be true to the mission of faithfully articulating the values of your innovation.

PROBES (questions/activities):

37. Rearticulation: Select and transfer/consider your most promising experiment (or simply any/each experiment). Restate it if needed.

38. Disruption: What approach does it disrupt? Be both concrete and philosophical.

39. World: Treat your experimental outcome as the product or exemplar of a new world. Speculatively articulate this. Draw, write fiction, diagram, get multimodal. The key is that your speculative fiction cannot lose the difference that you have developed during your experiments. Guard against falling back into existing frameworks, paradigms and worlds. It is better to be uncertain, have gaps in the story then to return to what exists and produce a known recognizable narrative. This articulation is a beginning and not an end.

- Name
- Description

40. Defining Issue: Considering your novel world — what would you consider its defining feature or features to be? Try to frame this as an issue or even a question. For example: the defining issue of classical Liberalism is: how small a State is needed to protect individual freedoms?

41. New Questions: What are all of the new creative questions that arise as a result of this world? Try and make an extensive list.

Speculate on how these might play out as actual practices, logics and even infrastructures.

42. Assemblage: What new areas of practice would be required by this world?

What experts would you need to consult? Make a list. Be as concrete as possible. Reach out to people. Talk with them. Visit labs. Bring them in for discussions. Develop research trajectories with them. Consider them part of your emerging community and commons.

43. Speculative World Model: Develop a diagrammatic model of your world using an X, Y diagram.

- Try making various versions by isolating two critical underlying variables
- Use this diagram as a tool to speculatively explore various zones, or possibilities about your world. Make these real experiments (fold them back into the practices and processes of the previous practice (Experimentation).

44. Speculative World Process: Make a process diagram of how things occur in a sequential manner. Be abstract and lay out a number of possible process diagrams.

- Test these by using them as instructions for action -- do they lead to novel and different results?

"I thought I had reached port, but I found myself thrown back into the ocean"

g. deleuze quoting g.w. leibniz

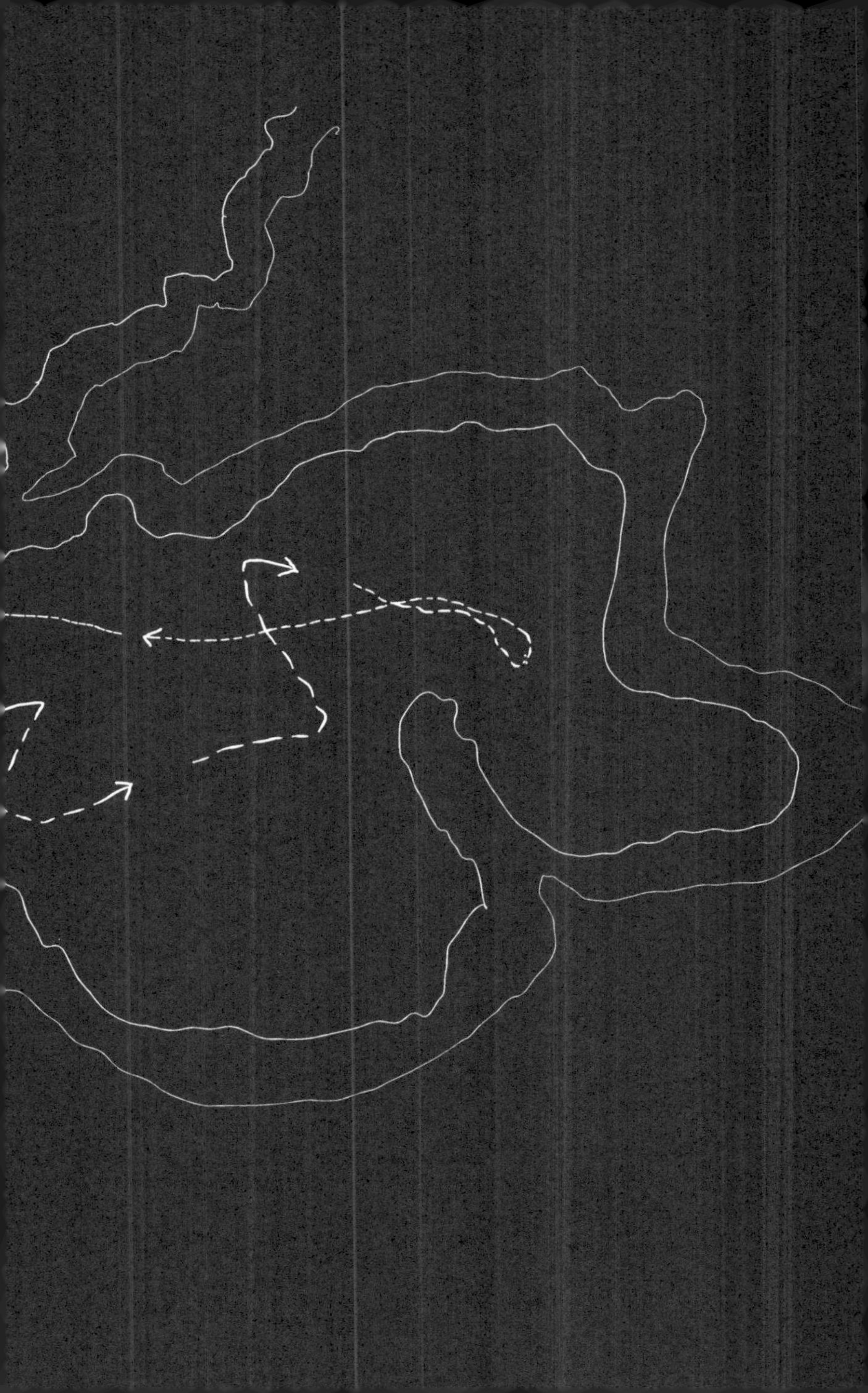

TASK: DEVIATE

PRACTICE: OUROBOROS: THE DEVIATION FROM THE DEVIATION

OVERVIEW

From personal experience we have found that it is profoundly difficult to develop a genuinely novel paradigm or world. Most often our first attempts still sound quite conventional and solution oriented. Because of this we developed a technique to help push a quasi-novel world into real novelty and qualitative difference. We call this the "ouroboros" technique after the famous snake that eats its tail. And true to this image, we are trying to make our world eat itself.

The technique is puzzling as it sounds: we ask of our world "how can you apply the job of the world to the form of the world itself?" This produces a paradox as an outcome — a question that cannot be rationally answered (much like a Zen Koan e.g. "what is the sound of one hand clapping?"). Answering this paradoxical riddle leads to a genuinely novel paradigm or world. And at which point we go through all the previous steps of worldmaking a second time.

This is by far the most challenging step for most people. It is very hard to leave our logic, rational problem solving and utilitarian habits behind. But the struggle is both critical and worth it — something astonishing comes from it (trust the process).

PROBES (questions/activities):

45. Paradoxical Inflexion: Apply the function of your world to the world itself. This is a paradoxical and illogical task. How do you apply the action of an object to the object itself? Try it. Describe. If possible, test.

- What comes out of this experiment? Do it a number of times.
- How does this change your world (it should make a qualitative difference). Describe.

46. Reworlding: Loop back through the previous practice of worlding. Answer all of the questions and do all of the activities. Keep doing this loop until you have developed a qualitatively distinct and interesting world

TASK: DEVIATE

PRACTICE: 11. STRATEGIC JOINING

OVERVIEW

Once you have developed a powerful and unique paradigm you need to develop a way for your paradigm to meet our existing reality in such a way that it can affect a genuine transformation.

There are two directions for you to go at this point: 1. Reconnect with your original question, or 2. Follow your new paradigm in whatever you decide is the most promising direction.

To do the former is quite simple: reconnect and map the direct opportunities. The latter is a bit more involved: it requires research: how does the existing reality look from the perspective of your novel paradigm? Where is the most opportune place for your new paradigm to flourish? Where is it "needed" most? It might not be anywhere near where you originally started. This is OK, let innovation lead you. That said you can choose to keep the focus on your original "area of concern" or you can put that aside and freely follow your novel paradigm.

Take your time to do this field work. Consult experts in the fields that you listed. Ask them about your defining issue. Explain what you are up to. Learn from them. But, most of all: keep your difference alive.

These two tasks are research oriented and speculative. They are only the beginning of how your novel framework can have a concrete transformative impact on our existing world. In this way they are a transitional phase, from developing a novel paradigm/world to making it concrete.

Develop a plan to move from a novel world towards concrete outcomes. From seeing the big picture you can strategically reorient your project. This is a question that you need to keep coming back to and revising: Where and how to meet the world?

This is not a question that can be answered once and for all — it will only emerge via a long history of engagements. Very often one does practices #9-11 repeatedly until something magical happens. Play the long game. Trust the process. From here forward it is all probing, testing, speculating and seeing what emerges. Work with others, develop a community, share tools, techniques, concepts, and outcomes. This phase cannot happen alone.

PROBES (questions/activities):

Part One: Internal Articulation

47: Speculative Model: Develop a speculative model. Diagram and outline the practices, and assemblage.

48. Internal Manifesto: This is not a public manifesto or argument to convince outsiders. This is a guide for the team to keep your difference alive as you progress. Write out as a series of axioms or principles. Take your time. Share widely. Pin up. Change as needed. Consider it a work in progress.

49. Trends & Connections: What is reality doing in relation to your novel world? Discover everything you can that might be of relevance to your novel world. Share widely. Keep your difference alive. Connect and develop your network as you do this research.

50. Immanent Ethics: What new modes of being ethical are emerging from your world? Don't shoehorn your world into an existing framework of ethics, allow one to emerge. Consider the questions below as general prompts. Fold your answers back into your internal manifesto. Test these ideas out. See your immanent ethics as a powerful creative act.

- In what unique way does your world empower some set of unique agents and environments?
- How will your world move some set of agents and environments towards new forms of well-being?
- How will your world account for its environmental footprint?
- How does your world engage with difference?
- How does your world engage with inequalities?

Part Two: Joinings

51. Novel Approaches: Write out all the key novel approaches, concepts, methods, techniques, tools, practices, environments, agents that have emerged from your world. Don't edit this list. Don't think about products or solutions — just make a massive list. Be broad and complete. And also consider going into more detail on any area that seems most promising.

52. Points of Impact: What are all the existing fields, activities, and practices that your approach could have an impact upon?

- What are all of the things that could be done in those fields, etc?
- Consider specific points of impact. Do the necessary research (this can be significant). Be complete.
- Consider how you are going to relate to the field that you originally began the innovation journey in. Are you concentrating on paradigmatically transforming this field? Or are you looking at other quite distinct fields? This is a significant decision and will shape the scope of how you move forward.

53. Diagramming Impact Strategies: Develop visualization and organizational tools to understand all the connections between your novel approaches and possible points of impact. Hierarchy diagrams work well to do this.

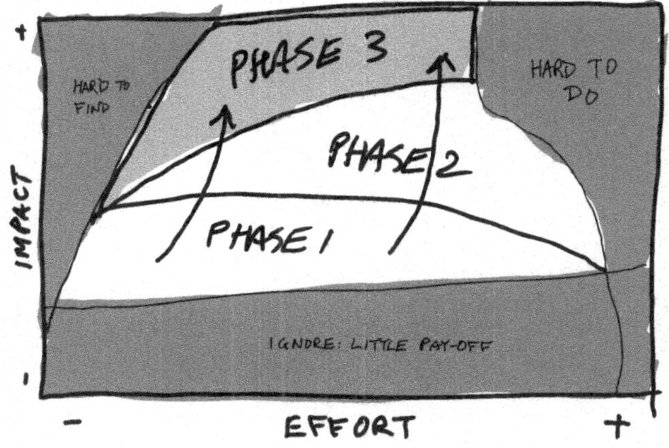

54. Relocate & Engage: Now you are developing a strategic plan of what to focus on. This is a big undertaking. This needs to come out of your deep engagement with the previous six questions. You will need to develop a strategy to come up with your strategy. One tool that we find extremely helpful is an Impact & Effort Matrix.

- Make a blank diagram
- Transfer every novel approach/point of impact to this diagram
- Then edit out the three zones: Hard to find, Hard to do, and Little pay-off.
- Look at all that remains along the upper edge and right side of the diagram. What is most interesting or promising?
- Connect this back to other related points in the diagram.
- Do these two steps for various options.
- Consider each of these as possible "future backward" strategies (with the future being the upper/right edge of the diagram).
- What do you have?

TASK: DEVIATE

PRACTICE: TEST

OVERVIEW

Testing Your Approach - The Review Presentation:

At this point in the development of your innovation it is critical to get feedback. The type of feedback you need is speculative, constructive, experimental, helps you develop the concepts, and most importantly keeps your difference alive — ideally it will help push your difference.

To get the most from feedback you need to present things in a thorough, concise manner that articulates the values, world and approach.

The other key aspect to getting great feedback is bringing in the right collaborators/strategists to review the work. You want people who know and care about the world, paradigm and values you are engaged with. Additionally you want to prepare them: *this is not a "critique" session* — it is not about evaluation (good/bad, like/dislike). You need constructive feedback that keeps your difference alive and pushes the project forward. Additionally you are looking to see if you missed something critical/creative etc.

Here is a list of what we recommend presenting:

- Paradigm
- What are you disrupting? (walk the group through your evolution: from the existing paradigm, to what you are blocking, to what you followed, to how this experimentally develops into your novel paradigm?)
- Diagram of where it meets our current reality in an interesting manner
- Choice: how you have relocated your practice
- Plan: what is your general plan?
- Project(s): what are the next projects/tests going to be?

Note: When presenting, take the feedback you receive very seriously and fully incorporate all of it into your plan. If you present well, in a constructive format, with the right people giving feedback — *what they offer cannot be ignored* — even if it is not what you want or expect to hear.

PROBES (questions/activities):

1. Presentation: Develop your "presentation". Focus on getting people to deeply connect and understand your world. This might take you far beyond any standard presentation. Consider immersive experiences and scenarios that might be critical. Get as much feedback as possible. Utilize a really good facilitator for this.

2. Review Notes: Make considerable notes. Divide into the following categories:

- World
- Ethos/Ethics/Manifesto
- Impact/Strategy/Opportunities
- Other

3. Review Incorporation: Spend considerable time with the feedback. Share it widely with your team and network.

4. Looping Plan: Develop a plan that takes you back into the previous practices and tasks.

5. Transitioning Plan: When the project is ready, begin to move to the next task.

task four

emerge

the encounter makes us

EMERGE

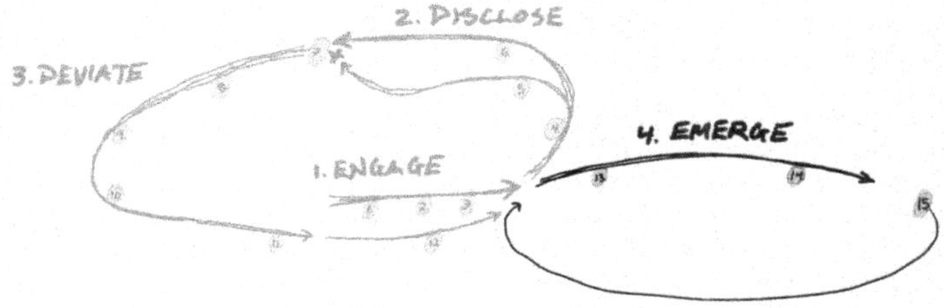

Entering the Emerge phase is not simply beginning another task in the innovation process — it involves the transition from the realm of disruptive change to the wholly distinct realm of developmental change. The world of disruptive change is one of big leaps and shifts to invent radical novelty, while the world of developmental change is all about continuity, incremental change and gradual improvement. The reason for this transition is simple: now it is time to make your speculative world real, and doing so requires entering the world of developmental change.

You and your innovation are crossing over from the universe of change-in-kind to change-in-degree and as such it is fraught with all sorts of unique difficulties. You are crossing a threshold from generating an aberrant speculative world and approach to the process of making this real enough to have a profound concrete impact. To negotiate this transition well requires a totally different set of skills and techniques than the previous phases required — and totally different skills than it will require to successfully make real world impact happen. The transition between change-in-kind and change-in-degree is its own unique activity.

Transition is a form of emergence where many distinct components align, interact and transform into a new state that is irreducible to any one component. This is a complex task where real world change happens.

The complexity is not the real challenge — that is always there no matter what you do — the real challenge is twofold: (1) to keep your difference alive, and (2) be comfortable with the fact that this phase is just as creative and open-ended as the previous steps. The need for creativity never ends.

Once you have negotiated the transition (practices #11 and #12) , new difficulties emerge and new skills are needed: it is time to realize some consequences of your new world *concretely* within our existing reality. This second part of the Emerge phase brings us to the sets of practices most closely associated with contemporary entrepreneurship (practices #13 and #14). This is for the simple reason that entrepreneurship focuses on fast and nimble strategies to bring things into reality. The other reason that we only now turn to these techniques is that none of the existing entrepreneurial methods have effective models for generating truly novel innovations, and thus they are best suited for working within the universe of developmental change.

Ultimately, there is no end to the ways one could approach this phase. Currently many models are taught and debated. All of these models strive to replace the classical business plan — that massive document that laid out all contingencies and planned the next five years. Such in-depth long term planning is a serious mistake from the perspective of innovation. Innovation, and all forms of newness, rely on open systems and emergent possibilities, long term advanced planning develops a closed linear model and as such makes innovation impossible. An in-depth five year plan closes off the possibility of unknowable-in-advance pivots, shifts, leaps and evolutions that are fundamental to all innovation.

Techniques such as the Business Model Canvas, Disciplined Entrepreneurship, Running Lean, Design Thinking, Equity Centered Community Design and Framework Innovation are often used for this. Each of these has unique advantages:

- Running Lean: very simple, quick process
- Business Model Canvas: a strong simple iterative model

- Disciplined Entrepreneurship: In depth focus on customers and connecting to customers
- Design Thinking: begins by surveying users for problems
- Equity Centered Community Design: powerful techniques to activate and address community
- Framework Innovation: good pre design analytical tools

All of these methods stress fitting ideas/products to actual needs and users with techniques like "customer validation." What distinguishes Innovation Design during the Emerge phase is that outcomes *co-evolve* with the evolution of "users," environments and the makers. Which is to say all parts of the process are mutually changing each other. This is a critical distinction. The new does not come into being by being forced upon users and environments. But neither does the new leave users and communities unchanged. Each is changing the other while refusing to fall back into the old world. This process of co-emergence is facilitated by (1.) treating novel ideas/products as probes and not prototypes; and (2.) iterating on the entire process multiple times.

A final note: It is important to recognize, just because we are making something concrete does not mean that creativity stops. It takes as much creativity, for example, to figure out novel economic possibilities as it does to design any other aspect of the process.

BEFORE YOU BEGIN

Each task of Innovation requires a different mindset and approach. It is important to prepare yourself so as to be fully present in a manner that is most conducive to the goals of each phase. Here are our suggestions:

- Transitioning mindset: an awareness of leaving one world and entering another
- Become more quantitative and developmental
- Find the dynamic middle ground between novel possibilities and concrete reality
- Trust the process (go step by step)
- Understand and believe in emergence
- Engage, solicit, and foster new collaborators — build and co-emerge with community
- Have a gardening mindset: cultivation and growth
- Have a systems focus (building capacity for change, networking collaborators, feedback, etc.)
- Hold onto your novel world — rationally keep your difference alive
- Build a self-sustaining ecosystem — not a cult of your personality, or personal vision

TASK: EMERGE

PRACTICE: 12. EMERGENT TRANSITIONING: CULTIVATING DYNAMIC CO-EMERGENCE

OVERVIEW

Whether you are starting at this phase or continuing on from the previous phase, the transition from disruptive to developmental begins by assembling and developing a network around your nascent world. The goal is to *co-evolve* what you are offering *and* a people for whom it is relevant. This might sound simple and obvious, but it is neither a one-way process nor is it black and white. You and your ideas will change and so will those who use them — you are co-evolving, small steps by small steps. If all goes well, the people you engage will transform from curious participants to collaborators, to users, to supporters, to customers. We call this "use generated design".

To do this we will do four things during this stage:

- Develop a call to engagement.
- Develop a concrete strategy to engage with communities (and why). Some of these people and communities will be experts, others potential users, and yet others are those who are super passionate about similar worlds, questions and approaches.
- Make a probe. A probe is a very simplified quickly produced tool. It should only have one key aspect or essence of what you are interested in. The purpose of this probe is to activate the field and allow interesting habits, practices, uses and transformations to spontaneously arise. This will require people to use and change your probe. Ideally the probe evolves in real time with many users. The probe is not your product, but what arises in these probes and tests should give you the critical insights to co-develop your product in the next stages of the process.
- Iteratively test and co-emerge (see above).

PROBES (questions/activities):

Part One:

53. Initial Vision Statement: Your initial vision statement is a direct outgrowth of the final work that you did during the task of Deviate. Now that you have developed a specific strategy, paradigm, approach, and area of focus, you need to translate this world/paradigm into a more focused and concrete form. Now it needs to reflect how, where, and why your project is meeting a specific area of reality.

- Articulate the area
- Why are you different?
- Paint a clear picture of the new approach
- Be speculative: what will happen when this approach takes place?
- Recognize that this statement will evolve and transform significantly

54. Operational Manifesto: In parallel to your Vision Statement develop an operational manifesto — this will be a type of internal guide to keep your difference alive at an abstract level while you develop very concrete outcomes. It should remind you why your novel world matters.

55. Potential Collaborators: Now that you have a new focused area of engagement, identify potential collaborators (specific individuals, communities, possible users, etc.). Be specific and make the connections, and begin to fold them into you project (see part two below).

Part Two:

56. Trends: Continue to research trends that both support and hinder your projects evolution. Do this in collaboration with your evolving network. Look beyond general trends to emerging or even forgotten technologies and practices that would be of critical importance. Fold these in.

57. Minimum Viable Probe: At this point teams, especially entrepreneurial teams develop an MVP — a minimum viable product. This is a mistake, it is far too early for products. (Another example of what is done is a Pilot Project — also a rehearsal of the final product. But the impetus to make and get something in peoples hands is right. We like to call this a Minimum Viable Probe or a Pirate Project. The goal of this is to activate some specific environment and community to initiate a co-evolutionary process of emergence. This process will allow a community, an assemblage, and a set of tools to co-emerge. As Gilles Deleuze likes to remind us, "The foundation can never resemble what it founds ... it is of another geography, without being another world."

- Minimum Viable Assemblage: What is the assemblage that is necessary for this probe/pirate project?
- Location: What is the right location and group of collaborators (community). Perhaps there are several.
- Test: Develop a scenario that you will use as a "test". Do a few trial runs and improve.

58. Scenario Playing: Carry out the various engagements. Understand these as scenario playing for emergent co-evolution. Make sure you have a very light hand in these engagements. What happens? What do people actually do? What emerges? What keeps happening? Pay close attention, make good notes and do not try to defend your designs or approach — let things flow and go where they go. Interview participants before and after. Engage them with your vision. What is their sense of things?

Repeat Part Two a few times with distinct scenarios that evolve and follow what emerges that is most surprising, interesting, novel and supports your world/paradigm with each iteration

How to get good feedback when interviewing:

- Get out into the world (at the right time).
- Set up situations.
- Document. (Photograph, video, sound, drawings, diagrams).
- Take good notes.
- Don't ask yes/no questions.
- Take time. Figure out the right duration.
- Use observation.
- Let them extensively use the probe in as realistic a manner as possible.
- Don't over explain, or hand-hold — let people explore and take things in their own directions.
- Iterate on your interview methods. Research and test techniques. Improve.
- Beware of false positives and negatives.

Note: It is important to remember that you do not have a product, and "customers" do not exist. It is critical to remember that both the "product" and the "customers" need to be co-developed — co-emerge during the process of the Emerge phase of Innovation.

59. Co-evolutionary Developmental Outcomes: When the previous iterative process has co-evolved interesting results, it is time for synthesis.

- What conclusions can you draw?
- Should you move forward with something, or do you need to go further back in the process? And if you decide you need to go back — how far? Be open to going back to any point in the innovation journey.

If you are moving forward, the next step is to take some time to get things in order. Review and evolve your Vision Statement, Operational Manifesto, your collaborators, assemblage, etc. This happens in the next section:

TASK: EMERGE

PRACTICE: 13. COEVOLUTION (& STABILIZATION)

OVERVIEW

Now, at this moment is the beginning of being more public and less protective/sequestered with the innovation project. Up until this point you have protected your project from the everyday concerns about problems, solutions and outcomes. Co-evolution and Stabilization marks an important moment of transition.

The probes of the previous stage should have begun to evolve into a semi-stable ecosystem of engaged users, collaborators, fellow explorers, techniques, habits, tools, and environments.

Now you want to critically unpack this and learn everything you can from it. Begin by taking all the feedback and synthesize this by answering the questions "who engages." Some of these people will become key collaborators and even customers (early adaptors), but just as importantly others will be those who will feel threatened by your project. It is critical to consider what role these people/business/interests groups will play in the evolution of your project. They cannot be ignored.

With this done, consider what you learned from the co-emergence stage. Put all of this information into the worksheet: make notes, draw and diagram as needed:

- Consider carefully what you should do next in terms of your probe and research:
- Do you need to develop an alternative call to action, new probes and do the process again?
- Or perhaps it is a simple modification and then do the process again.
- Do people connect with your world? What is really causing the connect, or the disconnect. (This might be something quite unexpected).

Remember the purpose of a probe: it is a tool for testing, feedback, change and growth. *The goal is not to simply confirm that your "product" works and "people" want it.* You are developing your concepts in a co-evolutionary manner and as such nothing happens all at once. Take your time and co-evolve. Ideally this step will loop many times. Enjoy this back and forth, take pleasure in feedback and the surprises of how others use things. We often find that the ideal number of repetitions of stage 9 and 10 are around 40! So, while learning the process you might only do this phase once or twice —in reality you will be doing it many more times.

BEFORE YOU BEGIN

Each phase of Innovation requires a different mindset and approach. It is important to prepare yourself so as to be fully present in a manner that is most conducive to the goals of each phase. Here are our suggestions:

- Become even more quantitative and developmental
- Find the dynamic middle ground between novel possibilities and concrete reality
- Trust the process (go step by step)
- Welcome more collaborators
- Understand and believe in emergence
- Cultivation and growth mindset
- Have a systems focus
- Be iterative and let the process generate outcomes
- Listen deeply and transformatively
- Be self critical
- Care about the details
- Become a competent maker
- Understand equally every aspect of your emerging business and be creative in every aspect.

PROBES (questions/activities):

Part One:

The next step is to take some time to get things in order. Review and evolve your Vision Statement, Operational Manifesto, your collaborators, assemblage, etc. Once things are in order it is time to unpack what emerged in the Scenario Playing exercises:

60. Who: Start by reviewing your participants:

- Who are the early engages/adopters? Analyze and get specific. Develop abstract typologies. Who else would fit this? Connect. Where are they? What are they up to? What got them to be so engaged?
- Who are the key collaborators? Who emerged to be critical collaborators — playing a significant creative role in what developed? Be specific. Make sure they become a part of your team and ecosystem.
- Opposition: Who and what became significant points of contention? Why? Was it something intrinsic to the novel paradigm or was it something about the structure of the experiment? What does this opposition mean? How can it be a constructive aspect of innovation? Test. Engage.

61. What Worked: What key components of the experiments really worked (in relation to your novel paradigm/world etc.)

- Area of Interest:
- Benefit:
- Location:
- Novelty:
- Requirements:
- Language:

Part Two:

Here we shift from making catalytic probes to prototypes. The experimental scenarios will have revealed "what needs to be done". Practices, frameworks, services, products in their nascent forms will have emerged. What are these? List and describe.

62. Prototype: Develop actual prototypes for each aspect. Develop a plan to insert them holistically into a specific practice(s). Use a Minimum Viable Product methodology. Make numerous variations and alternatives.

63. Activation & Iteration: Test these. Iterate Parts One and Two. These iterations should be in close dialog with your Vision Statement and Operational Manifesto. All of these will co-evolve collectively with an evolving community of engagers.

The number of iterations of prototypes needed is usually over 40 at a minimum. More often it is 100+ This often surprises people. The key is to set up a system that allows for fast feedback and making. Work with multiple variations and distinct sets of variations. Explore boardly, fuse variations, and don't be afraid of dead ends. Diversity, multiplicity and evolution is the name of the game.

TASK: EMERGE

PRACTICE: 14. ECOSYSTEM BUILDING IN THREE PARTS

PART ONE: DESIREABILITY

OVERVIEW

Now it is time to move on to developing a "outcome/product" and its fit to a "need" and "market" — but only when you have a pretty evolved and stable ecosystem (users/collaborators/community, a shared worldview, practices, habits and tools)*.

This next practice begins to walk you through a series of questions to test and develop the viability of your endeavor.

*We put product, need, and market in quotes simply to note that you could, and should, define these in a very open manner.

PROBES (questions/activities):

64. Desirable Iterations: Focus on desirability — this is between your evolving vision statement + product and "customers". These customers should have initially co-emerged with your co-evolutionary process. Now you are looking to see that this can expand. Iterate to evolve this. Be specific and concrete.

65. Achievable Iterations: Can you actually carry out what is needed to make your outcome? What does that network look like? Who is making what by what means? Does this process really produce an outcome that is the one you and your world demands? Iterate to evolve this. Be specific and concrete.

66. Viable Iterations: What is the economics of this process and outcome? How can you invent unique ways to make this viable? Iterate to evolve this. Be specific and concrete.

67. Novel Iterations: Is all of this truly in keeping with your paradigm, world and vision? Iterate to evolve this. Be specific and concrete.

ECOSYSTEM BUILDING PART TWO:

USE GENERATED ECOSYSTEM EVOLUTION

OVERVIEW

When designing an outcome — whatever form it takes (physical object, a service, an app, a restaurant, a social movement) it is critical to begin the design process in such a way as to evolve your design directly with users. The design is generative. The "use generated design" process is counter-intuitive — you are not trying to put the perfect product out there and see if customers love it, rather you are giving users the simplest version of your idea that has only one key feature (this is often called an MVP, or Minimum Viable Product). The idea is to get transformative design feedback from the very beginning of the process. The generative process is iterative — each MVP generates design outcomes that leads to the next MVP, that leads to the next and so on. This is a process of growing your design with users and will take on average dozens of rounds of iteration. This might seem like a painful waste of time that would be better spent perfecting the design away from prying eyes and criticism and only then presenting it to the world.

Note: Starting from your prototype and the feedback you have gotten from it, design the next version of your product (remember this could be anything from a service, a movement, or an object). It is really important to keep iterating and making multiple distinct products. Your mindset for innovation at this point in the process should still be one where you are "in love with the problem and not the solution". There will always be more than one physical way to solve or address any questions. Make sure you are always open to diverse possibilities as you make.

PROBES (questions/activities):

68. Outcome Evolution: Develop and put in place an ever more actual user generated design process. Focus on

- Things
- Practices
- Taskspace
- Greater Assemblage

Iterate and evolve/grow the total ecosystem.
This should be the "launch" and the beginning of the actual life of your outcome.

ECOSYSTEM BUILDING PART THREE:

DEEP ITERATION

OVERVIEW

Now that you have worked through most of the Emerge Phase and developed an outcome, it is time to test this against your original ideas that came out of the Deviate Phase. This is a critical step where we can ask:

A. Novelty

- Did I keep my novelty alive? Is it still a difference that makes a difference?
- Is this project really pushing my novel paradigm?

B. Fit

- Is this outcome the best way to help the paradigm meet this reality?
- Is this outcome working? Should we try another possibility we mapped out?

C. New Novelty

- Has my outcome done something different? Is my outcome developing a new distinct novel world?
- How do I take into account this new world? Do I need to map this out to not be blind to the new possibilities?
- Is this new novel world more interesting, or an advance upon the previous world?
- Define and Explore

Take what you have done and test it against your world: go back to your paradigm and your mapping of how it meets contemporary reality. Be open to the real possibility that you need to rethink the outcome of the Emerge process.

Rethinking your outcome is a wonderful and necessary opportunity — it simply means going back through the steps of the Emerge Phase with a new speculative approach. Ideally, you would have the time and resources to take many approaches through this process in parallel prior to deciding with which to go forward.

Do this review in a similar manner to the previous review: Outside reviewers, formal presentation, and folding feedback into project. Present:

- Your Paradigm
- Your World to Contemporary Reality Fit
- Your Plan
- Your "Product"

Ask of your reviewers to use the above questions to guide their reflections and responses.

Note: Make sure you have the right type of reviewers and they fully understand what you are asking of them.

PROBES (questions/activities):

Follow the described logic above and carry out the process in two sprints:

69. Deep Iteration #1: Looping back to points in Emerge

70. Deep Iteration #2: Looping back to points in Deviate

Feed these directly into your stabilized and developing world/outcome.

TASK: EMERGE

PRACTICE: 15: AMPLIFICATION: PT. 1 ECOSYSTEMIC ROLL OUT

OVERVIEW

After doing the deep reiteration and review of your project and responding to the feedback in a concrete manner: now make a "final" version of your product. Obviously, this is no final version of your product — rather it is the "first" version of your product. It is the one that you can feel confident in releasing to the world and that can work independently of you in the manner it is intended.

Nothing exists on its own. Everything that exists only works and has meaning because it is intrinsically part of a network of other things. This ecosystem is critical to the success of your innovation — and ultimately will be your innovation. The car could only come into being with new roads, gas stations, a global infrastructure of mining (gas, metals etc.), new forms of factories, etc. The BMC is a reasonable sketch of this ecosystem, but it does not cover everything that is critical to developing a robust ecosystem.

Make a list of key components and diagram their relationships. Annotate this diagram. Determine (to the best you can) which are most critical and which might be the best opportunities. Follow up on these first. Develop.

PROBES (questions/activities):

71. Feeding Forward: Develop a robust ecosystem and network

TASK: EMERGE

PRACTICE: 15. AMPLIFICATION PT. 2 REPEAT AND EVOLVE

OVERVIEW

So you think your done — this process never ends. Begin again. Return through "zero" — the unknown — the null point and begin again

PROBES (questions/activities):

Back to zero...

put the ladder down

GLOSSARY

Affordance

A term from ecological psychology, used to understand things by what they "afford" a user in contrast to understanding a thing based upon its explicit purpose. Example: A glass bottle's purpose is holding liquids, but one can discover that it affords one many ways to make sounds from tapping to blowing across the mouth. By privileging things affordances we open ourselves to a vast space of unintended possibilities which are critical to innovation. Much non-human innovation emerges via unintended affordances (See: Exaptation).

What is critical is thinking about things not as what a thing "is" but what it can do. This is situational, relational and emergent. Because of this relation and emergent logic there is no end to the number of affordances.

See: Gibson, and Deleuze in bibliography.

Agency

The power of anything to affect and be affected by anything else.

Ambiguity

We are taught to believe that we can have clear and distinct ideas because reality follows a plan which must be clear and distinct. But most of life is profoundly vague, dynamic, slippery, chaotic, uncertain and blurred.

Novelty in its process of emergence is inherently vague and ambiguous. It cannot have any other state without being destroyed.

We need to not only welcome ambiguity but develop techniques to actively work within this condition. This indeterminate logic means that ideas are not the be all and end all of innovation. In fact ideas play a small role in the early stages of innovation -- they act as hunches -- provocations to experiments. Doing, making, following, co-evolving are all more critical in the early phases of innovation. Our cultural bias towards ideas is a huge handicap to innovation.

See: Hunches, Vagueness, Emergence.

Autopoiesis

Some things have the ability to make themselves. Much of our classical understanding falls apart because of a lack of understanding that not all things need a creator, plan or source. Autopoietic systems can generate order and even life from non-order.

Self-organizing systems under the right conditions will spontaneously generate order. Crowds will suddenly act in a unified manner, plants will grow in specific forms and inanimate materials will spontaneously take on certain forms all without any hidden regulating or organizing substrate (genes, rules, plans etc.). The emergence of novel worlds requires working within the logic of self-organizing systems.

Becoming

Non-developmental change. Change in kind where the "change" has no subject distinct from itself. A "block" of becoming. Opposite of development.

Blocking

Technique to stop repeating what is known. Creativity = not repeating what has already been done. Creativity is often mistakenly defined as "complete freedom" or "no rules" but that is not the case. Innovation requires strong rules to refuse existing rules, patterns, tools, habits and worldviews.

Blocking is a refusal and the beginning of a process of experimentation: "if we no longer can do this, what can we now do?"

Blocking, while it might sound simple or crude, is a sophisticated form of "enabling constraint". It enables a difference to be nurtured by constraining the norm, but only if the choice of what to block is well chosen.

Blocking is a nuanced activity that first requires knowing the existing rules patterns techniques etc. so that they can be effectively blocked. The key to blocking is to disclose an existing paradigm or world, and this is itself a phase (Disclose) of innovation.

See: Disclose, World, Rules, Enabling Constraint.

Betrayal

Paradigmatic innovation requires betrayal. Paradigmatic change is not an improvement of an existing world, but a total rupture. You will need to leave a world behind. This is a very difficult thing to do. You will feel deeply torn, uncertain and out of your depth. You will be judged as crazy, mistaken, dumb... On top of this you will have no guarantee that you are onto anything worthwhile. This state of being is not the same as being comfortable with failure. It is a deeply unsettling uncertainty that does not go away.

Care

Care for the event, care for the experiment.

See: Sympathy.

Chance

Chance is everywhere, and critical to everything -- all innovations surf chance -- innovators harness it. It is a wonderful method to remove classical forms of authorship. It has been well developed by artists and designers as part of algorithmic techniques.

See: John Cage, Olipo in bibliography.

Change

Change comes in two forms: change in degree and change in kind.

Creativity — Psychological

Confusion, assumes creativity is a thing that can be located in the brain of humans. Standard model.

Creativity

A process to develop novelty. Two forms: degree kind. Question of difference. Pure difference, differing.

'Creativity' is the universal of universals characterizing ultimate matter of fact. It is that ultimate principle by which the many, which are the universe disjunctively, become the one actual occasion, which is the universe conjunctively. It lies in the nature of things that the many enter into complex unity."
A. N. Whitehead

Crisis Thinking

A mindset that prioritizes urgency over a considered response: "Things are so bad that if we do not act now it will be a total disaster!" or "We need to act now, doing something is better than nothing!" This leads to a deepening of the problem rather than any solution. It is common in environmental issues such as Global Warming. Crisis thinking leads to dangerous feedback loops that escalate the problem: "See, we did not act soon enough or fully, and now the problem is so much bigger -- now we really need to act as big and quickly as possible!"

See: Solution Thinking and Thing Thinking for related conceptual framework errors.

Co-Evolution

This gets to the chicken vs egg paradox (N+C Paradigm). We can leave behind such logics if we carefully understand how complex systems participate in co-making. The thing and its environment co-make each other.

A process where you and the "thing" you are making shape and transform each other.
Both the "product" and the community of users come into being via this process. The key insight is, you are not making a product after which you will discover a community of "users."

The process of design co-evolves the users and the product in an iterative loop of co-development and co-specification. This process stands in deliberate contrast to ideas of "customer discovery" and "customer validation" or the prototyping process in design thinking.

See: Emergence.

Collaborator

Specific people + things + processes + paradigms + environments that you need to work with on any phase of a project. Critical is to realize that the agent of innovation is the collaboration (the whole).

Note: They do not stay with you for the entirety of a project, this changes with phases.

Confirmation Bias

It means that we always look for the evidence to support our views. On a deeper level everything we see, say and do in our everyday mode of attention confirms our views.

While this issue is well recognized, the real question is much deeper. We do not all live in the same neutral reality which we just see differently based upon our biases (or cultures or world views etc.).

This model of diving reality into (1) the really real and (2) interpretations is itself flawed.

See: World, Reality Divided, Data Blind.

Context

Being sensitive to context is not the same as assuming that context is a case of following a set or contextual rules (general to particular). Nothing is reducible to history or context. Becoming is irreducible to history/context -- these are necessary but only that. what they can do/become is an open question.

See: Emergence.

Data Blind

Your observations undermine the possibility of your worldview, but you cannot see it because your worldview is so strong.

Deficit Model

The belief that people only lack info and if they had it they would act.

Design

The process of making. Both human and non-human. Both material and immaterial. At many scales.

Over the last century the term "design" has referred to the making of things, and the term "designers" has referred to those who make these things. (Usually these are useful things as opposed "non-useful" things which have been historically categorized as "art".)

Critical here is that design as a term and as a field is much broader than the making of concrete objects. Design is a process to shape movements, transform systems, develop concepts and make things. This needs to be taken further, design as a process is not just reducible to human practices. Design is the process of making -- whether human or not. This is important for many reasons, not the least of which is that human making is always embedded in larger and smaller non-human processes. It behooves the human designer to understand that they are part of multiple other non-human processes.

Design Thinking

A user-centered design strategy that is a form of developmental design. Focus is on empathizing with users and asking about their problems and needs. Steps: Empathize, Ideate, Prototype, Make.

A popularized model of various engaged and user-centered models of design, all of which have real advantages over historical models of Direct Design. While empathizing is important, Design Thinking is not an effective method to develop disruptive or paradigmatic innovations. Additionally, by being an "ideate first" process it has all of the pitfalls of direct design in terms of developing any form of real novelty.

See: Making.

Development

A step by step process of improvement. A change in degree, not kind. Opposite of becoming.

Developmental Design

Forms of design that are best suited to development vs qualitative change. User Centered Design and its variants (such as Design Thinking) are good examples.

Deviate

Phase of the Innovation Design process.

Difference

Change. Normal assumption is that difference comes after identity: difference is a change. This is only a difference in degree. Pure difference is a difference that precedes identity: no copy model or origin. Two types:

1. difference in degree
2. difference in kind

Difference in Degree

Difference in kind when pushed across a threshold.

Difference in Kind

Small changes or iterations.

Direct Design

Best understood as the "fallacy of direct design". Historical model of idea driven linear design (illusion). Ideate--Model--Make.

Innovation: "as in actual life, we make detours, we go by side-roads. We see the straight highway before us, but of course we cannot use it..." Wittgenstein.

See: Developmental Design, Responsive Design.

Disclose

Phase of the Innovation Design process.

Dynamic

Nothing is static, everything is process -- fields and processes. Stability is the temporary dynamic state of one phase of a system. Feedback loops will tip the system into another state. The set of these linked states or phases produce a type of meta-stable condition. Movement is form coming into being (without necessarily following a plan).

Emerge

Phase of the Innovation Design process.

Emergence

Process of Innovation comes about not via some mysterious or mystical internal process but via the process of emergence. Emergence is the technical term for a process of coming into being that exceeds and supersedes its inputs. Smaller events/components come in unpredictable manners that are irreducible to the logic of the component parts. It is a form of non-linear and non-incremental change (change in degree).

Emergence: This process is the key to all forms of creativity that avoid the N+C Paradigm. It is how something seems to emerge from "nothing". It is the process by which the new emerges from the old. In the most simple terms: it's the process by which things emerge that are:

1. Greater than the sum of their parts.
2. Irreducible to their parts. And...
3. make their own parts.

There are many examples of emergence all around us -- that we are conscious beings -- is a classical example of emergence. Consciousness is something that requires having a brain, but is irreducible to the brain, and it changes the brain. Why does this matter for creativity? We so often understand making as a process of addition. We add parts together and get a whole (Think of how we assembled things with Lego as a child). Here the parts make the whole and the whole can be taken back apart and each part can be analyzed to understand the whole. This is a reductive model of making. We can reduce the final product to the parts and the process. Cars can be built this way. But the genuinely new does not come about in this manner.

Empathy

In distinction to Sympathy. Component of sympathy. More than psychological.

Engage

Phase of Innovation Design

Enaction

Way to understand a being's relation to their environment and how they co-create and co-enable each other. Developed from Cognitive Psychology. Understands humans (or any other being) to be embodied, embedded, extended, enactive and affective. Critical alternative to the classical view of human-world relation.

Enabling Constraint

A term Erin Manning & Brian Massumi coined for rules that limit actions to enable novelty.

See: Blockage & Rules.

Escalation

Much of our solution oriented thinking that ignores the systemic nature of reality tends to escalate the very issues it is trying to address.

E.g. addressing hunger by sending surplus grain to Africa has led to the collapse of farming as prices are held artificially below what is sustainable for an african farmer. This is usually the outcome of taking problems to be objective.

Event

Always excessive. There is always more than. Seed of newness.

See: Exaptive

Equity Centered Design

Inclusive form of community design

Exaptation

This is the evolutionary process of utilizing the unintended consequences (affordances) of a physical feature to novel ends. Most, if not all, critical features of organisms evolved in this manner: wings, eyes, bones etc.

Darwin originally called these phenomenon "preadaptation," but this suggests that the creature was somehow preparing for this novel features emergence (that it could know in advance about flight). Recently, Stephen Jay Gould and Elizabeth Verba proposed that this be called: exaptation, because it is outside (the ex part of the term) adaptation. Which is a beautiful way of describing creativity -- it is a process of novelty that is outside of fitting into any existing purpose.

See: Gould in bibliography.

Excess

Creativity relies on the excess of each and every moment, thing, process and event.

Experiment

How do we do things experimentally? Stop asking "what is it?"

In terms of creativity it does not matter "what it is." What matters for an experimental approach is: What can it do? This is curiosity in a nutshell -- to keep asking of things and events, what else can it do? And what else can you do? This can only happen by doing -- not just thinking. Things will surprise you when you push them beyond their supposed purpose. (Your chair is a tool for scraping and these glorious scraping sounds are the beginning of a new musical genre...).

Things will rupture your comfortable assumptions about what they "are" (they are, in fact, doing it all the time -- we just choose to ignore them). Asking "what is it?" sends you back into the past and the known (the dictionary of good and proper definitions). "What can it do?" ask you to put things into new contexts, environments and connections -- into creative play -- now you are in the middle of a relational and experimentally open question.

Explaining Away

When novelty -- a difference -- first emerges it is quite fragile and prone to be mis-recognized as what already exists. It is very hard to see difference as a difference.

Two dangerous but very common habits that erase difference is [1] our tendency to Universalize, or [2] reduce things to a form of Utility.

See: Universalizing, Utility-as-the-answer.

Idea

Never at the origin of newness and radical creativity. The cause of the new is never an idea. the idea/conceptualization of the new comes later — often much later. It is both a serious conceptual error to posit an idea at the beginning of an innovation and a methodological error in developing an innovation design process.

See: Intention, Direct Design, Design Thinking, Emergence, Enaction.

Immersion

Synonym for the Engagement Phase of the Innovation Design process.

See: Engagement.

Indirect / Non-linear

Disruptive innovation. Non-prediction. Innovation: "as in actual life, we make detours, we go by side-roads. We see the straight highway before us, but of course we cannot use it..." Wittgenstein.

Innovation

Differences producing difference via threshold searching and crossing.

Innovation Design (Approach)

Design process for activating creative and innovative potentials in any context. Consists of four phases: Engage, Disclose, Deviate, and Emerge.

See: Design, Engage, Disclose, Deviate, Emerge, and Immersion.

Intention

Creativity surfs the productive gap between intention, and use, engagement, or actuality.

Making

Making as thinking

Matter of Concern

More general and abstract way to articulate an initial "problem". key to avoiding "solution thinking."

Map

Not a representation of the terrain but a tool to engage with the terrain.

Mediator

Transducer.

Newness Paradox

See: Innovation Paradox.

Open

Seems like such a simple term. Open means that every final closure or summary is simply another "thing" beside everything else in the system. Open relates to all of these terms. Open does not mean "anything goes", but it is quite a wild and disturbing term. When you are finished the winds come in from the open to expose you to what happens next -- for which we can never be ready... Perhaps the only source of great joy or humor.

Paradigm

Mindset -- goals, rules, structures and parameters arise.

See: World.

Paradigm shift

Fundamental change in kind

Play

Putter, tinker.

Problem

Easily misunderstood as "something to solve or overcome". Well stated problems already include all possible answers. A further misunderstanding is that innovation is focused on how one solves problems. This is wrong. Innovation is at its most creative when it invents new problems.

Problem-Solution Coupling

Interdependence between a problem and its solutions.

Probe

Not customer validation. Rather, co-evolve moment.

See: Co-evolve.

Process

Reality is composed of processes. Nothing is simply a discrete object. Everything comes into being via a process, stays in existence via another process, and transforms out of being via yet other processes. To innovate is to see, think, and live processes.

Proposition

A proposition is the articulating of a tendency sensed in an experiment (event).

Relations/relationality

The fixed state of all things. Things are always connected and one could further state that [1] the connection (relation) is a thing in itself, and that [2] "things" are their connections.

See: Emergence.

Realism

A call to be "realistic" -- a claim that change is necessary but real change is "unrealistic" -- very common call around issues of global warming or climate change.

Romantic Creation

That creativity is the absence of conditions and rules. Determinism vs negation. Idea vs spontaneity. False choice.

Solution

Solutions are “answers” to a problem. Problems are really ways of posing a question. Any question determines a possible field of answers. Thus solutions never come alone and are ultimately only as good as the question being asked (along with its underlying assumptions).

As designers/makers we often fall in love with our solutions (answers). This is a mistake (from the perspective of creativity). We need to fall in love with the possibility of becoming the creators of problems worth having.
See: Problem, Problems Worth Having.

Solution Thinking

taking a problem and all of its implicit assumptions for granted and only focusing on solving the problem as it is given. Leads to very limited forms of innovation and most often a repetition of the underlying issue.

Systems

Set of elements or parts coherently organized and interconnected.

Stakeholder

People you cannot ignore. Those who are part of the ecosystem of your matter of concern. (This is not an ideal term.)

Success Bias

This is also related to what is called in systems thinking: success to the successful. It is really easy to fall into the trap of rewarding what has succeeded so far -- painters know about painting and so they reward what they know -- it goes for race, forms of transportation, and so on.

Sympathy

"What things feel when they shape each other."

See: Things, Bibliography: Sypbrok.

Tendencies

During experiments the field often self organizes around certain spontaneously emerging tendencies. These are cues towards possible novel emergences.
See: Experimentation, Following, Event.

Thing

An active x. Things are not passive nor are they our intentions.

Thing Thinking

A belief that the world is composed of discrete things and not systems. The desire to see everything as a thing (e.g. creativity). Corrective: systems thinking, dynamic systems theory (DST).

See: Emergence, Systems, Process, Feedback and Feedforward.

Transformation

A worldview without creativity. Anthropological turn.

Tuning

Creativity requires attunement. We do not begin as "authors" or "makers" -- we begin by tuning ourselves to the rhythms of a novel event. One needs to develop a very serious practice of creating a mode of attunement.

Universalizing

A problematic process for ignoring or denying differences that matter. "We are all the same..." Additionally a problematic answer to questions: we should all aspire to the same solution--a classical model of this is all of the Western answers to social questions: Development, Capitalism, Liberal Democracy -- as if this was the sum total of all humanity's possibilities.

Unintended Consequences

Or consequences. There are only consequences (See: Intention). Creativity utilizes the unintended. All newness is part or wholly unintended. In this manner we cannot write-off unintended consequences as negative, for they are wholly productive and edging into the new.

Utility-as-answer

Habit of explaining any situation or object via "utility". This is a common form of world-blindness. Universal explanations.... to make useful or to fit into the past. The trivial and the useful are not distinct from the perspective of making.

World

All thoughts, ideas, concepts and practices necessarily depend upon a space of implicit "pre-understanding." This pre-understanding hangs together in a holistic manner. Implicit set of embodied practices, environments, ecologies, tools and mentalities (mindset) that ground and support a way of seeing, understanding and engaging with reality.

Can be very general (e.g. the "western" worldview) or can be more specific (e.g. Plus the habits, and the physical systems that support and reinforce this.)

World Making

Experimental process of making a world. Key process for innovation. (See: World). An event self coordinating and coming to value. Never done. Never plug and play -- you cannot "switch" worlds. Speculative -- for a people still to come (Deleuze).

Worlding

Synonym for worldmaking

World Blind

Not able to see that things are always of a world. Being world blind is most often a condition of innovation: in making something radically new it is very difficult to see that it is the harbinger of a totally new world (paradigm).

Being world blind is only a problem if one cannot transition out of it to sensing the novel world / paradigm. Most often innovators are too close to their innovation to sense the world that they are ushering into being.

Note: Opposite: Data blind: Your observations

undermine the possibility of your worldview, but you cannot see it because your worldview is so strong.

X The unknowable that fringes all action with radical possibility.

ABOUT US

Jason Frasca - **Founding Partner**
Jason is a native New Yorker — born and raised in the New York City metro, worked in and around every borough, and pretty much seen everything the city does from the back of his motorbike.

Really from birth, Jason has been an urban innovator, sleuth of futures bubbling up in the sidewalk cracks, and anthropologist of everyday lives.
Since childhood Jason has been hacking systems and imaginatively speculating on alternative futures — he likes to say that he was the family innovation consultant by the time he got to preschool. These formative experiences led him to become an entrepreneurial business executive, marketing, and sales professional managing Fortune 500 and nationally recognized clients in many diverse sectors of the economy from direct marketing, non-profit, entrepreneurship, startups, private investigations, insurance, and international law. In each of these sectors, he brought systemic and transformative innovation that combined astute trend analysis and the right level of disruptive envisioning to push companies into blue ocean spaces.

Because of his unique approach and diverse experience midway through all of this Jason was recruited to higher ed to become part of the core faculty to invent a new entrepreneurship and innovation program.
He envisioned and brought the first maker space to a school of business and began a renaissance in how entrepreneurship, innovation, and design are taught in business schools.

From being a pioneer to now part of developing a movement to transform innovation education in general Jason has put people, the planet, and meaningful innovation at the heart of his approach to teaching. On almost any given day Jason can be found collaborating with colleagues deconstructing complex problems and providing a systems design approach to the collective invention of new possibilities. In his role as an academic Jason has worked on program-level curriculum development, invented new ways to teach students via intensives, international retreats, immersive travel programs, long-term mentorship, and transformed the infrastructure of the school.

From those rough and tumble days in New York City to the innovation consultant of today Jason has dedicated his career to designing radically innovative technology solutions and processes for companies, communities, and ecosystems with a visionary and pragmatic mindset that has yielded massive results with limited resources.

Iain Kerr – **Founding Partner**
Iain is a west coast kid who grew up in a very different Vancouver in an era of visionaries and dreamers. He remembers the sailing of Greenpeace boats and summers swimming in the harbor. He spent years climbing mountains and this deep immersion in the wilderness led him to research philosophy, ecology, complexity science, and evolutionary theory and convince him of the radical power of being generalist for innovation and creativity.

Those formative years led Iain to become a designer working at the intersection of creativity, ecology, and emergent systems — always with the goal: to make novel worlds possible. His unique approach evolves from over twenty plus years of experimenting across and beyond the zones of Architecture, Design, Ecology, Art, Creativity Studies, Ethnobotany, Food Studies, Systems Thinking, Social Entrepreneurship, Commons Studies and Philosophy. His focus when working as an innovation consultant is on designing novel collective processes to transform seemingly intractable problems into, as he put it "problems worth having for worlds worth making".
Like Jason, Iain was brought into start a new entrepreneurship program at Montclair State University, where together they are Co-Director's of the MIX Lab (Making and Innovating for X). The MIX Lab's mission is to foster innovation at all scales.

In addition to co-directing the MIX Lab, Iain is a co-founder of the boundary-blurring design consultancy SPURSE and the Emergent Futures Lab.

SPURSE has been at the forefront of ecological research, experimental design, and innovation leadership for the last 15 years. While developing ground-breaking ways to probe, catalyze, disrupt and re-imagine systems both large and small, they have collaborated with communities, organizations, and individuals from the high arctic to inner cities neighborhoods in Bolivia. Their award-winning projects reveal an astonishing range of creative solutions to effecting real change: from restaurants, wetlands, wayfinding apps, urban renewal programs, microbiology laboratories, cookbooks, buildings, everyday tools and more.

In 2018 Iain and Jason Frasca founded Emergent Futures Lab as a platform for the rethinking of creativity, invention, and change — what they are, how they are realized, and how they can be taught. The Emergent Futures Lab has developed a number of new tools including the Innovation Design Approach.

Iain regularly works as a consultant, lecturer and workshop leader on creativity, innovation, and design (MIT, Harvard University, Columbia University, Parsons, Yale, CCA, and RISD). His most recent research is on developing new models of Innovation that are collective, enactive, materially engaged forms of novel worldmaking: Innovation Design. His and SPURSE's work has been discussed in books and journals from the NYTimes, ID, and Surface to The International Encyclopedia of Human Geography.
Now as Iain looks back from his early days hanging off a cliffs ledge to exploring the coasts of British Columbia he finds the similar adventure and joy in carrying out the work of Emergent Futures Lab internationally.

Emergent Futures Lab
A strategic innovation consulting firm.

Some refer to us as "Blue Sky" consultants. That stuffs us into a box. We don't like boxes. We prefer to tear the box up and create entirely new spaces of possibility. Because our award winning innovation program is about more than just creating product differentiation and inventing new markets.

We help make all types of innovation happen.
From co-evolving new paradigms to developing transformative innovation cultures. We are passionate about evolving existing products and services in unintended novel ways, and how we can use radical innovation to meet our 21st century challenges from social to the climate crisis.

The fact is, we get fired up about one thing:
How to Innovate

Sure, we spend our free time deconstructing innovations to understand where and why products, services and markets evolve and flourish while others wither into irrelevance. But what gets us up every morning is working with people, communities, and companies to innovate meaningful possibilities.

Let's connect and innovate something beautiful together,

Iain Kerr: iain@emergentfutureslab.com
Jason Frasca: jason@emergentfutureslab.com

Want to learn more? Visit our website:
emergentfutureslab.com

Acknowledgments

This book has been many years in the making.

Over the last two decades the research and the development of the big ideas/practices behind this project were carried out in the field by members of the design collective SPURSE.
From there we have developed, tested and refined various models and formats — going through countless versions for different projects and classes. Everyone we worked with in this process, especially students and community members, has had a critical and creative role in shaping this for the better.

Since 2017 we have been collaborating with the entrepreneurship team at the Karl-Franzens University of Graz, Austria. Our colleagues there have had a formative hand in making this what it is.

At our academic home base: the MIX Lab @ Montclair State University, the whole team has played many important roles. We thank each and everyone of you — you have shaped this, and us, for the better.
Thank you.

wonder
discordant
adventure
unknowable
next

NOTES

Made in USA - North Chelmsford, MA
1317003_9781737673200
06.08.2022 0859